THE DIRTY REALISM DUO

CHARLES BUKOWSKI AND
RAYMOND CARVER
ON THE AESTHETICS OF THE UGLY

Borgo Press Books by Michael Hemmingson

Auto/Ethnographies: Sex, Death, and Independent Filmmaking
Barry N. Malzberg: Beyond Science Fiction
The Dirty Realism Duo: Charles Bukowski & Raymond Carver
"Give Me the Gun," She Said
Hold Me, Please, and Say This Is Love
How to Have an Affair and Other Instructions
In the Background Is a Walled City
Judas Payne
The Rose of Heaven
Seven Women: An Erotic Investigation
Sexy Strumpets and Troublesome Trollops
The Stripper: A Tale of Lust and Crime
Vivacious Vixens and Sultry Sluts
The Yacht People

Books for Other Presses

The Naughty Yard (Permeable Press, 1994)
Crack Hotel (Permeable Press, 1995)
Minstrels (Permeable Press, 1997)
The Mammoth Book of Short Erotic Novels (Carroll & Graf, 2000)
The Mammoth Book of Legal Thrillers (Carroll & Graf, 2001)
Wild Turkey (Forge, 2001)
The Comfort of Women (Blue Moon, 2002)
The Dress (Blue Moon, 2002)
My Fling with Betty Page (Eraserhead Press, 2003)
Drama (Blue Moon, 2003)
The Rooms (Blue Moon, 2003)
The Lawyer (Blue Moon, 2003)
House of Dreams Trilogy (Avalon, 2004)
The Garden of Love (Blue Moon, 2004)
Expelled from Eden: A William T. Vollmann Reader (Thunder's
    Mouth Press, 2004)
Short & Sweet (Blue Moon, 2006)
William T. Vollmann: Freedom, Redemption, and Prostitution
 (McFarland, 2008)
Star Trek: TV Milestone (Wayne State Univ. Press, 2009)
_Gordon Lish and His Influence on 20th Century Literature: The Life
    and Times of Captain Fiction_ (Routledge, 2009).
The Reflexive Gaze of Critifiction (Guide Dog Books, 2009)

THE DIRTY REALISM DUO

CHARLES BUKOWSKI AND RAYMOND CARVER ON THE AESTHETICS OF THE UGLY

by

MICHAEL HEMMINGSON

The Borgo Press
An Imprint of Wildside Press

MMVIII

The Milford Series
Popular Writers of Today
ISSN 0163-2469

Volume Seventy

FIRST EDITION

CONTENTS

PART I: THE DEAD & THE DIRTY

1. What the *Fuck* is Dirty Realism? 11
2. Two Dead Writers 16
3. The Small Press: On the One Time I Met
   Bukowski 22
4. The Elements of Dirty Realism 42

PART II: BUK

5. The Los Angeles Novel 49
6. Suicide Notes on a Proposal for a Book 66
7. Guilt and Grace: How Charles Bukowski Dealt
   with His Fame And Fortune 72
8. Post-Kafka: On Bukowski's Cockroaches 97
9. "Some Picnic" 101
10. "Carver on Bukowski" 103

PART III: RAY

11. About Dirty Realism: A Meditation on Carver's
    "Gazebo" 109
12. "I've Seen Some Things": Parental Grotesque
    and the Sex Lives of Mom and Dad 138

13. Re: "A Serious Talk" 142
14. Re: "What We Talk About When We Talk About
    Love," a.k.a "Beginners" 146
15. Why Do You Ask? Interrogatories 151
16. Deciding Issues: Carver on the Body of the Infant
    and the Entrapment of Fatherhood 155
17. Domestic Violence and Child Abuse in American
    Fiction: A Critical Meditation on Carver's
    "Popular Mechanics" 162
18. Two Final Quotes 177

Bibliography 178
About the Author 183

For

Jolene and her imaginary friends:

Toby, Murgatroy, and Gertrude—
the dirty [un]realist trio…

All fans of Buk and Ray

I have been digging my grave from the instant I was born.
---William T. Vollmann,
    Riding Toward Everywhere

They dragged me down. Down the muddy hill with me frantically digging in my heels....
---Jack Gilbert
    "From These Nettles, Alms"

PART I.

THE DEAD AND THE DIRTY

THE DIRTY REALISM DUO

1.

WHAT THE *FUCK* IS "DIRTY REALISM"?

C ertain critics have categorized Raymond Carver as a founding member of the Dirty Realism literary movement.

What is this term?

Dirty Realism showed up in the early 1980s, branching out from minimalism, the stripping of fiction down to the least amount of words and a concentration on the object. The characters are usually run-of-the-mill, every day people—the lower and middle class worker, the unemployed, the alcoholic, the beaten-down-by-life.

Charles Bukowski is considered by many critics to be the godfather of this sub-genre, followed by Carver.

Granta #8, published in 1983, was devoted to "Dirty Realism: New Writing from America." Editor Bill Buford describes Dirty Realism as "a fiction of a different scope—devoted to the local details, the nuances, the little disturbances in language and gesture" (4) relegated to the short story rather than the novel. Dirty Realism is

unadorned, unfurnished, low-rent tragedies
about people who watch daytime television,
read cheap romances or listen to country and
western music. They are waitresses in roadside
cafes, cashiers in supermarkets, construction
workers, secretaries and unemployed cowboys.
They play bingo, eat cheeseburgers, hunt deer,
and stay in cheap motels. They drink a lot and
are often in trouble for stealing a car, breaking a
window, pickpocketing a wallet (4).

In other words, fiction about the common person, but
unlike the "common man" of Updike, Mailer, or Malamud.
Granta is a British publication; in that respect, Dirty Real-
ism appears to be a European term for the study of ordi-
nary American life as represented by extraordinary Ameri-
can fiction.[1] *Granta* 8 includes work by Carver, of course,
Richard Ford, Tobias Wolff, Frederick Barthleme, Bobbie
Ann Mason, Elizabeth Tallent, and Jayne Ann Phillips.
Granta 19 (1986) is devoted to "More Dirt: The New
American Fiction" and offers, again, Richard Ford and
Jayne Anne Phillips (who must be double dirty), Joy Wil-
liams, and Robert Olmstead as practitioners of the form.
Neither volume includes Bukowski, which is a curiosity, if
Bukowski is indeed the alleged Dirty Realist godfather.[2]

---

[1] Bill Buford is an American, though. A note about who he is and why he
can claim to define Dirty Realism — he edited *Granta* for sixteen years
and was *The New Yorker*'s fiction edition from April 1995 to December
2002. He has published the bulk of the most important contemporary
short fiction writers, American and European.

[2] I am not going to jump to any conclusion, that *Granta* may have refused
to acknowledge Bukowski's work as many academics have in the past,

Granta 8 includes Carver's "The Compartment," a story from his final collection, *Cathedral*. I question its use as a correct example of Dirty Realism, as defined by Buford. The story is set in Europe, about a middle-aged American man, Myers, taking the train to see his son, who is studying abroad. Myers is unlike the typical Carver male—he is not unemployed, a drunk, or reckless; he works as an engineer, stays in four-star hotels, and has purchased an expensive watch in Rome to give to his son as a gift. The fathers in Carver stories such as "Popular Mechanics," "The Father," and "Jerry and Molly and Sam" are young, frightened, unemotional—not ideal patriarchs. Myers does, however, recall an incident that reflects what is expected from a Carver character:

> The last time Myers had seen his son, the boy had lunged for him during a violent quarrel. Myers's wife had been standing by the sideboard, dropping one dish of china after the other onto the dining room floor. Then she'd gone onto the cups. 'That's enough,' Myers had said, and at that instant the boy charged him (69).

This passage is the only paragraph in "The Compartment" that fits *Granta*'s criterion of Dirty Realism. There are two dozen older Carver stories that could have been published

---

determining it to be "low culture" writing. There could have been publication rights issues—Bukowski's publisher, Black Sparrow Press, was known to be extremely protective of where their star writer's work appeared outside the scope of their editions. Perhaps Bukowski did not care for the term Dirty Realism—being the anti-academic he was—or *Granta*. There could be many reasons.

that better fit the parameters[3]—to start, "Fat," Carver's lead story in his debut collection, *Will You Please Be Quiet, Please?* It is a first-person narrative that concerns American diners, American food, and American obesity. The narrator tells his friend, Rita, about serving a big meal and elaborate desert to "the fattest person I have ever seen" (3). For several pages, he describes, in minimalist detail, the variety of foods the fat man consumes, one after the other—a Caesar salad, soup, bread and butter, lamb chops, and "a baked potato with sour cream" (4). "Fat" is not about observing the Other but concerns the narrator's desire for change in a life that is stagnant.

> That's a funny story, Rita says, but I can see she doesn't know what to make of it.
> I feel depressed. But I won't go into it with her. I've already told her too much.
> She sits there waiting, her dainty fingers poking her hair.
> *Waiting for what?* I'd like to know.
> It is August.
> My life is going to change. I can feel it (8).

The narrator, while finding the other man repulsive, is envious. The fat man is from Denver, he's from somewhere

---

[3] Again, as often is the case with publishing, the choice may have been a matter of what was available. Carver was not a prolific writer. *Granta* may have wanted a new story that was not widely read by Carver's audience. *Cathedral* had not yet been published when this issue was released. A magazine is cognizant of what makes an issue attractive for customers to buy: new work, rather than older work available in an author's popular book, or widely anthologized. Nevertheless, "The Compartment" is still not a good example of Dirty Realism.

else, he's traveling, he can afford all that food; he can eat and eat and indulge himself, not caring what others think. The narrator confesses that he eats a lot and never gains weight. "I'd like to gain," he says (7). He wants to be different; he wants his body to change. The fat man is free while the narrator, like Rita, is trapped in a meaningless job, poverty, geographic location, an unchanging body. What *is* Rita waiting for? Nothing; she has no ambition, does not understand the true reason why the narrator has told her this account—while the fat man can expand and transform, he simply remains the same.

This is the essence of Dirty Realism as practiced by Carver: blue-collar American lives so filled with ennui that it takes an incident of the seemingly grotesque, a social oddity, for a person to reach epiphany. "My life is going to change," the narrator in "Fat" states, because he *needs* to alter the monotony that has imprisoned his being.

Bukowski's Dirty Realism is too obvious—the drunk, the unemployed, the hopeless—does it get any more lower middle class American than that? The difference is that Bukowski finds humor in it all. I think a lot of new Bukowski readers are attracted to the low art nature of his work, but fail to see that Bukowski's characters have accepted their fates and condition; Bukowski is not making fun of them (or himself) but having a good time with it. Why bemoan it all the way Carver's characters often do? The Carver character hopes for better days, waits for them; Bukowski's characters know there won't be better days ahead and so they live it the best they can in the moment.

2.

TWO DEAD WRITERS

Heinrich Karl (later Henry Charles) Bukowski, Jr. was born 1920 in Andernach, Germany, the son of Henry Bukowski, a U.S. soldier, and Katharina Fett, a German citizen. His family emigrated to the United States in 1922, settled in Los Angeles. This is where Bukowski spent most of his life; the city became an integral part of his writing.

Bukowski's father was in and out of work during the Depression years, regularly beating the boy. Domestic violence was something Bukowski knew well. Back then, it was deemed appropriate for a parent to raise a child in home of physical violence. His father was a hard drinker who also abused Bukowski's mother.

After graduating from Los Angeles High School, Bukowski studied for a year at Los Angeles City College, taking courses in journalism and literature. He left home in 1941, apparently after his father read his stories and threw his possessions onto the lawn (as chronicled in *Ham on Rye* and various poems and interviews). Bukowski, however, still returned home when he was broke and on the streets.

During the war years, Bukowski lived the life of a wondering hobo and skid row alcoholic. He traveled across America, working in odd jobs: petrol station attendant, lift operator, lorry driver, and an overman in a dog biscuit factory. He had published a few stories in journals. His first sale was to *Story* magazine. He began to write poetry when he was thirty-five, and nearly died when he was hospitalized for alcohol poisoning.

This life parallels the life of Carver.

Raymond Carver was also an offspring of the working poor. His father, Clevie Raymond Carver ("C.R."), rode the rails from Arkansas to Washington State during the dust-bowl days of the 1930s. C.R. became a saw filer in the lumber mills; he was also a raging alcoholic who died at age fifty-three. Carver's mother, Ella Casey Carver, was no stranger to domestic violence either; she supplemented the family income by working as a waitress and retail clerk.

Raymond Clevie Carver, nicknamed *Junior, Frog, and Doc*, was born May 25, 1938 in Clatskanie, Oregon, a logging town, pop. 700, on the Columbia River. The family returned to Washington in 1941, and Carver grew up in the Yakima Valley.

Carver married at nineteen and fathered two children by the time he was twenty. Juggling "crap jobs," fatherhood, and eventually "full-time drinking as a serious pursuit," he managed to find precious time to write. "Get in, get out. Don't linger. Go on," were the bywords of his life. This lack of free time dictated the direction of his work—poems and stories rather novels or longer forms.

Much biographical information has been previously published about both Bukowski and Carver that there is no need to rehash what is easily found elsewhere. You've picked up this book for a reason, so you already know a lot about the lives of both these writers. I am going to assume you admire them, or are researching a paper or study; otherwise, why would you be spending your own precious time with my words and pages. In various chapters, I will discuss biographical matters as it pertains to certain novels, stories, and poems.

This introductory chapter is to point out some similarities in both their lives, which is the impetus for my writing this critical monograph. They are both California writers; although they were not originally born in the state, they each called it home, and most of their work is set in California or was inspired by life events that happened there. They have both been labeled as the original "dirty realists"—a literary category for certain types of American literature of the 1970s and '80s. They were both hard-drinking alcoholics and were hospitalized due to excessive drinking. Carver quit consuming booze in 1977 after nearly dying, and Bukowski switched from prose to poetry after nearly being killed as well, but continued to drink until his last days (albeit expensive wine rather than cheap wine and beer). Drinking and relationship issues arising from drinking were common themes of their mutual literature, which is a leading aspect of Dirty Realism. They both wrote about blue collar work, poverty, hopelessness—all the ugly things in life esoteric, literary writers from who sit in the Ivory Tower shy away from. Bukowski wrote about bad bowel movements, Carver about suicide attempts; these are life issues one would never see in the

18

work of John Updike or Bernard Malamud at the time. Both found recognition and initial "literary fame" around the same time in the late 1970s. They knew each other; they were acquaintances and read each other's work.

Bukowski and Carver are the most imitated contemporary authors of the twentieth century, especially when they were alive and at the top of their careers; yet traces of their influence can still be observed in the work of published, even famous and renown writers of today, and what is coming out of the plethora of writing programs, and what is landing in the slush piles of editors, agents, and publishers. For this reason, serious critical studies are useful, if not mandated.

Bukowski and Carver studies are on the rise—every year, new books pop up on the shelf, and articles appear in academic journals, taking one jargon-filled approach or another—Third Wave Feminist, post-structuralism, deconstructionist, pop culture, blah, blah, blah.[4] Both writers are studied in the classroom, both writers have been adapted by Hollywood.

Both, however, have not been studied together—this monograph is unique and the first of that kind. While this is a work of literary criticism, I am not following any one school or approach; call it "experimental" criticism if you wish, as I mix autobiography with discourse. If it must be labeled, call it "critifiction" as coined by Raymond Federman (see the meditation on "Gazebo," for further information, so I won't be repetitive here). This book does not

---

[4] One of the very best dissertations to be published in G.P. Lainsbury's *The Carver Chronicles* (2004), which I cite frequently from in this monograph.

follow a unified style—"Guilt and Grace" is presented in the form of poetry, or simply broken lines. In "Suicide Notes on a Proposal," I offer a standard book proposal for a study on autobiography and auto/ethnography in Bukowski's poems, stories, novels, and letters, aimed at the growing Life Studies and Studies in Autobiography fields cropping up within the rhetoric and writing divisions of universities...it seems to me that everything I have to say on the matter is said in the proposal, as well as individual chapters on this monograph, so why write a whole book on it. You will get the gist of my argument within the proposal form.

It should be noted that the style, method, and presentation of this monograph would probably not be acceptable within a traditional university or academic press, nor would I want it to be. The Milford Series: Popular Writers of Today and The Borgo Press, have been kind enough, and confident in my work, to accommodate my quirky critical approach. One of the finest works of literary criticism is D. H. Lawrence's *Studies in Classic American Literature* (1923). Lawrence stuck his nose up (and flipped the bird) to the conformity of critical methods of the time (as he did with all his work), forgetting the romantics and the New Critics, choosing an energetic approach rather than a stuffy, structured one. Basically, he talked about literature that mattered to him (Hawthorne, Melville, Poe) and why. *The Dirty Realism Duo* models itself after Lawrence's method and approach.

This book should also be taught in classrooms about twentieth-century fiction, Carver, Bukowski, and minimalism. It should be in every university and public library in the country.

Note that an institution does not employ me; I do not teach or profess or instruct. I am an "independent researcher" for the label, a writer for the spirit. I do not research and write literary criticism for promotions, tenure, to get or keep a teaching job, as 93.7% of the published critics do (this is an actual statistic). I write for myself; I study and research subjects that obsess and interest me, my life, and my other work. I approach criticism the same way I do novels, screenplays, short fiction, poetry, or the personal essay. *The Dirty Realism Duo* is written first for my personal edification, and joy, and second as a contribution to the current body of published Bukowski and Carver studies, as well as studies in twentieth-century fiction. It is my hope that other scholars, and students, will find this work useful for future research, discovering insights on these two writers not covered by other critics, and finding new meaning to what Bukowski and Carver have with their own lives, and why.

What is most important when studying the work of writer such as these is this: identification and reflection. The reader sees him or herself, their lives, their history and future, in the words and sentences; this is why Bukowski and Carver have been elevated to important, vital, necessary, popular—and above all, American—masters of contemporary letters.

3.

THE SMALL PRESS:
ON THE ONE TIME I MET BUKOWSKI

I noted in the previous chapter that many writers have, and still do, imitate Bukowski, mostly his style of poetry. Hundreds of would-be Bukowskis have written about drinking, whoring, hangovers, sex with the wrong people, and being down-and-out, whether they have experienced this or not. This is usually the MO of young male writers, sixteen to twenty-five, that discover Bukowski, Hunter S. Thompson, and Henry Miller, and are so inspired, so enthralled, that they want to be *just like* these writers. I speak from experience here; I know the route. When I first started publishing poetry and stories in the small press, older writers would admonish me that Bukowski was not a good role model, everyone wrote like him, and it was not an advisable life. I didn't listen. Bukowski was famous and rich, women threw themselves at him, surely he must have the perfect life—what did I know of being homeless, in the drunk tank, having health problems, having depression issues. Today, I say the same thing to younger writers: "It's cool and fun to read about a life like Bukowski's, but it's no fun living that life—it's sad, disgusting, lonely, heartache of an existence."

Some Bukowski imitators are simply frauds, pretending to be down and out but maintaining $80,000 a year jobs at universities. Other writers, such as Denis Cooper or William T. Vollmann, have led Bukowskian lives and experiences, to an extent, but make good use of the past, writing about it, to warn others of the pitfalls. Most Bukowski imitators never leave the space of the small press, never become well-known writers, and toil in obscurity forever, disillusioned that the chapbooks and small magazines read only by a few hundred people, if that, are contributions to American literature. Again, I am writing from experience, as I have, and still do, publish half of my work in the small press.

When I was a teenage small press poetry rag publisher and editor, I saw just how many Bukowski wannabes were out there—about the same amount of housewives who wrote cheesy, flowery verse or the young suicidal women who fancied themselves the next Sylvia Plath, composing lines and stanza about broken hearts, horrible men, miscarriages, and being lot in a post-feminist world.

Publishing a small zine was educational. The following is from an essay I wrote, appearing in the Winter 2007/08 issue of *ZYZZAVA*.

1983-85: Had an ordinary, dull childhood: youthful parents—mom and dad were in their late teens when they had me, but didn't get together, officially (as in living together and married) until I was five. Brother was born when I was ten and I was no longer the only child. The first word my brother said was an attempt at my name: "Gago." The four of us were housed in suburban Spring Valley (the "east county" of San Diego) where, like many bookish and loner kids, locked myself into my room and read about adventures in the novels of Jack Kerouac, Ernest Hemingway, and Norman Mailer. Read Joyce Carol Oates too, so it wasn't all male authors (I liked her short stories but could never get into her long-winded, repetitive novels, and her Black Sparrow Press stuff was better than the Trident Press stuff). Came from a regular, mundane lower middle-class background: my dad worked in construction, going from job to job, and my mother worked for the phone company, handling office paperwork. Wrote my first novel at the age of ten—a *Star Wars* sequel, 300 lined pages in a notebook, via pencil. That's how I got into reading and then writing: Star Trek. My buddy K.C. was a book nerd and lent me his copy of George Lucas' *Star Wars* novel— K.C. recently tracked me down on the Internet and mailed me that book, with a note: "This is what started you on that wrong path."

Got my first typewriter at twelve. Started to write a body of awkward and naïve novels, short stories, and po-ems. I mailed them out to places like *Isaac Asimov's Science Fiction Magazine*, *Heavy Metal*, and *The Paris Review*. The rejected slips started to show up in the mail when I was expecting big fat checks (even fifty dollars would have been a fortune to a kid). A "we're humbly sorry we can't use this" slip from *Harper's* had a note on the back of it, handwritten in curly scrawl: "Send this to the little poetry mags." What were those? I picked up

Writer's Market and found out (that many were out of business by the time the book was published).

Had my first poem accepted when I was thirteen and in seventh grade; it was ten lines of fluffy verse, taken by *The Archer*, a letterpress offering out of southern Oregon. Payment: five dollars and two copies. Was jubilant, convinced I would be the next Charles Bukowski, Richard Brautigan, or Jim Morrison by the time I left high school. Next poem was in another Oregon journal, *Dog River Review*, beautifully typeset on fine linen paper; the third was *again* from Oregon, *Taurus* (what was with Oregon?) that published the finest poetry of them all—the editor read submissions the day he received them, rejected or accepted (in a handwritten note on a subscription flyer for the zine) immediately. It was created on a manual typewriter, Xeroxed, folded, stapled, with an alleged circulation of 300. The publisher was a fellow named Bruce, I forget his last name, and his editorial note stated that volunteers from a senior citizens center would collate and staple each issue, each copy lovingly handled. When *Taurus* went from a manual to electric typewriter font face, I didn't think it looked right. There was something about the Olympia courier font that gave *Taurus* a real underdog, underground, reckless feel—the IBM font seemed so rigid, as if coming out of a business office.

Next was a publication out of Bakersfield, *Amelia*, paid ten dollars. *Gargoyle*, *Gypsy*, and *Impetus* accepted my work—Impetus Press, from Stow, Ohio, even issued my first chapbook, *Reaching into the Wet Darkness*, when I was seventeen. (I have seen, online, rare booksellers pricing the thing at fifty dollars.) *Gypsy* was published by Belinda Subraman (and is still around) by way of a military base in Germany. I wondered how many small presses were coming out of army, marine, or air force bases—*Gypsy* was the only one I knew of, but I'm sure there were others. *Gargoyle* was the most impressive of them all: each issue was professionally typeset, several hundred pages, perfect-bound, and it looked different each time out; editor/publisher Richard Peabody aimed to have every issue resemble an established, bigger literary journal. One issue looked like the *Paris Review,* another the *Kenyon Review*, another was in audio format, another was a mass-market-sized paperback of fiction only. Peabody also published books under the banner Paycock Press. I remember him telling me that *Gargoyle* was published on maxed-out credit cards and his co-publisher at the time, Gretchen Johnson, worked as a gourmet chef and made decent money that could be channeled into underground American literature. Peabody was the first magazine editor to write me detailed critiques on my short fiction, comparing my work to other authors or films, and explaining why he was rejecting my submission. To this day, I still publish in *Gargoyle*'s pages (it is a Print of Demand journal now) and have had work in Peabody's commercial press anthologies such as *Mondo Marilyn* and *Mondo James Dean* (my first published novella).

Decided to become a small press publisher when I was sixteen, my junior year in high school. Many of the poetry and "literary" scene zines, composed on typewriters, were printed via Xerox and saddle-stapled. I had published something like 150 poems in numerous little magazines by my junior year. Maybe it all began—this desire to edit and publish at a young age—my freshman year, when I was given the position of editor-in-chief for the school's creative writing annual. This was Mount Miguel High, in the suburb of Spring Valley in San Diego. Being head honcho of the creative writing annual was usually reserved for a senior, but the English teacher in charge, Mrs. Mott (who had once been a staff writer for the TV shows *Perry Mason, Mayberry, RFD* and others) was impressed that I told her I knew Harlan Ellison (my aunt lived next door to him in Sherman Oaks), even more so when I showed her my published poetry and acceptance letters (that I kept in a proud binder) for poems yet to see print.

Was also publishing short stories—*Samizdat* and *Wind* were printing my prose pieces, which never seemed to get past 2,000 words. *Samizdat* was run by a Marxist radical out of Berkeley, Merritt Clifton, who had a notorious reputation for being blunt and insulting in his interactions with writers and other publishers. When I mentioned anal sex twice in different submissions, he wrote: "Talk to you shrink about fucking women in the ass, not me." *Wind* was a modest, typeset little mag that was always over 100 pages, filled with poetry and fiction, and published by way of a farm in rural Kentucky. For some reason, *Wind* never rejected me; I never sent poetry there, just stories, and the stories were printed.

Samizdat Press published my second chapbook of politically-oriented poems, Nowhere is Safe, in a co-publishing deal: Clifton would supply the ink and the paper, I would pay for the manual labor (five dollars an hour, slightly more than minimum wage) to have some "kid" typeset and saddle staple the chapbook. The cost on my side was a mere thirty-five dollars, which I got from my grandmother in Los Angeles. Clifton told me he printed 400 copies for his subscribers, sent me twenty-five copies, and gave me my first ISBN, which appeared in Bowker's *Books in Print* the next year. Keep in mind that I was still in high school and this was an important step. Samizdat Press had a curious way of operating; I'm surprised others have not followed suit—subscribers paid for pages, not issues. A subscriber could pay for 300 pages, 500, 1,000, even for a lifetime. The pages would consist of irregular of the magazine, chapbooks, broadsides, even novels, whatever Clifton felt like publishing. sixteen of those pages were my chapbook, which can be found in several rare book rooms of university libraries (UCSD and University of Madison-Wisconsin) and, apparently, was translated without my knowledge in South America—ten years after its publication, a colleague (and poet) showed me the copy of my Spanish chapbook he found in Argentina.

Back to being the editor-in-chief of the creative writing annual—I wasn't the best editor, in terms of managing the core group of readers and production crew. I had started getting into alcohol and smoking pot and dropping acid the second half of the year, and I had never been in charge of anything in my life. I almost got my ass kicked for being who I was. This one fellow, who thought he was the school's greatest writer, this hard-core rocker with long hair and always in Black Sabbath T-shirts, confronted me after school one day. He had some buddies backing him up, as well as a couple of stoned, slutty-looking girls hanging around waiting to see a fight. He wanted to fight me because his stories and poems were not accepted in the annual. "You're afraid of my talent," he said, "you're out to ruin me, because you know my shit is the best shit anywhere, so now I am going to kick your ass."

Didn't feel like fighting. I was afraid to fight, of pain. I told him his submissions had never "crossed my desk," to speak in the vernacular of editors, and I had never seen them. Had he submitted them right? "I would have remembered them," I said; "I'll look for them in another pile, maybe a mistake was made, there's still some time to get new work in, especially excellent work like yours."

"Oh," he said, now sheepish; "oh, okay."

He backed off.

Was lying, of course—his writing, in my opinion, was pure self-centered crap, and it was too late: the annual was at the printer's.

What else? Oh yes—I got a blowjob out of my position. One of the readers was a junior and she took a liking to me. I thought she wouldn't be interested in a freshman, so I told her I was also a junior. She liked my writing, "you have style," and one day, in her parked car, we made out and she went down on me. When she found out I was a freshman, she was, naturally, very mad, only because I lied: "I wouldn't have cared what you are," she said, "except a damn liar."

A mimeographed oddity called *Occasional Review*, out of San Jose—generated by Ric Soos—was a great influence on my decision to start my own press. *Occasional Review* was just that, it didn't have a schedule, there could be two issues a year or six; its pages published my poetry, short fiction, and the interviews I conducted with various small press luminaries such as Ron Androla and Lyn Lifshin; each page was crammed with unruly, literate rants and book reviews. One that sticks in my mind is Soos' review of *Factotum* by Charles Bukowski, which he read (after having a fight with his girlfriend) sitting in the bathtub and falling asleep, he woke up and discovered the book in the cold, soapy water and he had to finish reading it water-damaged. There was something so "small press" about that image that stuck in my head. Soos also published books under the banner Reality Studios; several were by San Diego community college professors with side identities as poets, such as Don McClain, a sociology professor whose Reality Studios mimeographed chapbook, *When You See the Buddha on the Road, Shoot It!,* was the epitome of micro-press excellence for me—I read it over and over and, of course, coveted having my own chapbook published by Reality Studios—or *a book*, which almost happened: Soos had a short novel of mine but never came up with the money to print it as planned. That could have been my first novel. In my mind, at the time, even a cheap book with a few hundred printed copies scattered across the country meant Success with a capitol S.

Via mail, Soos mentored me in how to start a magazine—he wrote out a diagram how to lay the pages out, in even numbers, so that when folded and stapled, they chronologically made sense (I came to understand that this was the same method to make bound books—a traditional hardcover novel, for example, is comprised of a series of chapbooks, or signatures, sewn together and glued into a spine); he advised me on how to get the name out there, to solicit people for work, to get people to subscribe. Most of all, he said: "Do you really want to do this? Ask yourself why. What are you getting out of it and will it be worth it?"

There existed a peculiar network of small magazines with circulations of 200-500 copies, all communicating through the U.S. mail via publication, with names such as *Planet Detroit, Smudge Review, Poetic Justice, Northern Pleasure, Thunder Sandwich, Random Weirdness, Wormwood Review.* In many ways, this scene was akin to mail art; it formed a proto virtual community where poets addressed each other through stanzas; they held feuds, grudges, love affairs, and engaged in gossip about one another via prosaic broken lines deemed as verse. Was the scene incestuous and nepotistic? Was it any different in the academic press, the commercial press, the music or art scene? Soon, I found myself communicating on the phone with other writers and editors across the country, talking the talk of the small press, putting voices to the "pomes" (as some called it) I had been reading; I was having epistle relationships with men and women from Alaska to Italy to Wisconsin. When I was nineteen, I flew out to Detroit to participate in a brief romantic exchange with a woman twelve years older than me. She had published in *The Atlantic Monthly, Rolling Stone*, and *Kenyon Review*; and of course had her own small magazine. Almost daily, we wrote to one another (pre-email, of course), sent each other our work, photos, dreams, needs. If I didn't get a letter from her, I felt depressed and wondered if she was writing to someone else, and I'd get jealous. She told me in one letter, "I think about you and I making love." I replied, "When I go to Detroit, let's have sex immediately, right there in your car in the airport parking lot. Let's get it out of the way, so it won't be awkward. We won't discuss it, debate it, worry about it." She told me her last boyfriend had raped her on the kitchen floor after they broke up and she really needed tenderness, she needed someone to gently make love to her, and she said she knew I could do that for her. (Several years later she married a small press editor I introduced her to; he published her and later took her to bed; when they moved in together, they were afraid to tell me, thinking I would feel betrayed. I didn't care. I didn't go to the wedding. By that time, I was out of the small press micro-world.) Later, she even guest-edited an issue of my zine, once I got it started....

Started off with broadsides: single sheets of thick paper folded, devoted to one poet. I called the publication *Nuclear Café*. I called myself (for any small press publishing outfit is a person rather than a business entity) Mofo Press. *Nuclear Café* went from broadside to eight-page chapbooks. I was listed in Judson Jerome's poetry column in *Writer's Digest* and within weeks, hundreds of submissions poured in from all over the country, all over the world. My parents were annoyed, flabbergasted, but supportive. The mailbox in front of the house was crammed each day and the mailman sighed every time he came by (submissions poured in for eighteen months from that listing, as every small town writer's newsletter across the heartland listed it). When there was a new or substitute carrier, my mail would wind up with the neighbor next door (a cocaine dealer and a drummer in a glam rock band, with women constantly stopping by for five or ten minutes) or the neighbor across the street (the local busybody, that every street has, who would "accidentally" open some envelopes and read the poems people sent me); they would show up at my door with anywhere between ten-to-fifty pieces of mail, saying, "Wow, you must be popular!" I didn't explain because I didn't expect them to understand. What sixteen-year-old with long hair and acne runs a small literary journal out of his little bedroom and the house garage? "Normal people" cannot comprehend such a thing—they would probably say I needed psychiatric help, and they would have been right in that assessment.

What *does* make a person start a small magazine? From the old days of mimeograph to today's bright and risen technology of desktop composition and Print on Demand? Soos had a point, asking me what did I wish to get out of such a venture. The answers to these questions are for another time and another essay, perhaps going the academic route and taking an anthropological or psychoanalytical (Freudian or Lacanian?) approach; perhaps interviews with two or three dozen former and current small magazine editors/publishers is called for, to gather data for a sufficient ethnography on the curious creature known as a small press maverick (or madman).

Did I publish a zine for recognition, to contribute to contemporary American literature? Was it out of boredom or a need to participate, to understand that I was not all alone as I sat down at my typewriter…?

Nuclear Café was composed on my IBM Selectric and printed in "editions" of 100 via the photocopy machine in the office supply store at nearby Lemon Grove. It was paid for by whatever money I could scrape together; that and with postage, it was a tad pricey for a kid without a job (and no real desire to get one). A few subscriptions came in, though, and several desperate poets burning to see their name in print offered to foot the bill.

Wanted to publish something more standard, forty plus pages, with fiction and editorial asides, similar to *Taurus* or *Occasional Review*. A small press veteran in San Francisco, who published *The Second Coming Review*, suggested I procure a mimeograph machine to cut down the expenses. *Occasional Review* was done on a mimeograph and I loved that feel, that look—*not to mention the smell of that ink! Samizdat,* and my chapbook, were mimeographed. I talked my parents into buying me a used hand-cranked mimeograph for seventy-five dollars. I had printed flyers on the high school's mimeograph, which was a lot better than the one I had, but I knew how to prepare stencils, I knew how to load ink and deal with the sheet-feeder. There was a lot of trial and error, working late at night in the garage, drinking stolen beers from the fridge and changing *Nuclear Café* from a Xerox rag to a work of mimeo art, homage to the golden age of underground literary efforts. I would emerge from the garage at 4 A.M., covered in, and stinking of, *ink*, feeling like a true classic publisher.

Needed a name for the new zine. I asked around for nomenclature advice. *The San Diego Review? The Spring Valley Review of Contemporary Poetry?* One poet said: "That's all we need: another fucking review."
I had my name!
Another Fucken Review.
A.k.a., *AFR* for the U.S. mails and *Writer's Digest.*
Was a senior in high school when issue #1 came out. But my mimeo clunker couldn't handle that many pages, so I went back to the Xerox machine. Sometimes I would use the high-end copiers, gratis, at my mother's workplace when she went in on weekends to take care of backlog and there was no one but her inside the downtown office. (I later learned that a quite a few small magazines were published on the sly by people who worked in corporate of-

fices or the printing departments of insurance companies. In many ways, that was the perfect way to distribute underground literature: make the man pay! Snub the establishment!)

One day I got a bunch of short, weird, sexy poems from a woman named Cheryl Townsend. There were enough for a chapbook so I told her I would devote issue #3 to her poems, as an eighteen-page chapbook. We decided on the title An Ordinary Girl. It was her first chapbook, her first serious attention from any small magazine. She was an attractive woman in her twenties who said she was married to a sugar daddy ten years older than her; all she did was sit at home and write. Must be nice, I thought. An Ordinary Girl was my bestseller; I had to keep printing copies, sold perhaps 700, which wasn't bad. She, too, later became a small press publisher (and still is) of *Impetus*, that first published Sherman Alexie. Since I had inspired her, I have always felt Alexie owes me one.

The mail submissions doubled. Reviews were favorable. I would get the usual every-six-weeks overstuffed envelopes from Lyn Lifshin and Gerald Locklin, two masters of the mass attack—little nag editors will know what I mean. I had 100 subscribers by issue #3. And then one day, an envelope arrived with Charles Bukowski's name on it, postmarked from San Pedro. I thought it was a joke. But no: it was the real Bukowski all right. No cover letter, just five poems shoved in the white envelope with an SASE. I was so floored that I didn't have the courage to write him back. I just wanted to hold the sheets of paper that my biggest hero had typed his poems on, and took the time to lick stamps and drop into the mail. I had read somewhere that he still continued to send his work to "the littles" and how they were a curse and a blessing to him; he said he could never forget what they'd done for him but he hated them and yet still sent his work out notwithstanding.

Was now a small press regular and did not want to remain there forever. I was writing novels and mailing them out to publishers large, medium, and small. There were so many false starts and possibilities that it makes me cringe—it gets to my heart of hearts, a sit were—to still think about it. There was the short novel with Reality Studios, but before that, there was St. Martin's Press; at thirteen, I had submitted a 210-page science fiction titled *The Alien Man*. It was about an astronaut whose body is possessed by the soul of a dead alien on the moon, partially inspired by the astronauts-gone-insane novels of Barry N. Malzberg. Several months later, I received a letter from Thomas Dunne, a senior editor at St. Martin's who now has his own imprint. Dunne wrote that he really liked my book, it needed rewrites, but he wanted to take it to the editorial board for a vote. "I will get back to you soon," he signed off. He had no idea he was communicating with a kid in the seventh grade. I had no idea what to do with the letter. I didn't dare show it to my parents, they wouldn't understand; I was afraid they would have the same reaction as my English teacher, a hopeful writer herself, whose jaw dropped to the floor (really!) when I showed her the letter. She said, "I don't understand. Is this real? What does it mean?" I believe she thought I had forged the letter; she shunned me in class for the rest of the year.

St. Martin's Press never published *The Alien Man*. Waited for six months, turning fourteen. Had dreams about the novel seeing print. One day, my father said I had a phone call from St. Martin's Church. "Why is a church calling you?" he said. It was Thomas Dunne's assistant in New York. I held my breath, waiting for the good news. "I'm afraid the board declined to make an offer," she said.

Thought I was going to die.

"Mr. Hemmingson? Are you there?"

"Yeah."

"Mr. Dunne would be more than happy to read anything else you may have," she said.

Those words haunted me for months: "The board declined to make an offer." What a way to say "no." To this day, I loathe the word "decline."

Vowed to get St. Martin's to publish one of my books some day. I sent more in over the years. I published stories in several of their anthologies, and a novel with Tor Books, in the same offices and distributed by St. Martin's...to this day, I still plan to sell them on something before I head six feet under.

Applezaba Press in Long Beach contracted me to write a critical biography of Gerald Locklin. Applezaba published Locklin the way Black Sparrow published Bukowski. I happened to mention it to the publisher and the next thing I knew, I had a contract and a $100 advance, half paid on signing. My first book?! It was never written. Locklin was amused, flattered, but uneasy—he didn't think it was time for a biography, he said his life wasn't all that interesting, having spent the majority of it inside the academy. Applezaba never asked for the advance back, but it was my first book contract.

Next was Doubleday, at nineteen. An editorial assistant found my manuscript to an angst-ridden novel of sex and dismay called *The Lizards of October*. She wanted it to be her first acquisition, and told me it would not be easy, she had to show the project around and get in-house support. Another six-month wait went by. She called and said that reactions were mixed and ultimately her boss did not get behind her to support her bid to buy the book from me. Her boss, by the way, in true form of irony, became my literary agent many years later (and still is). When I told him about *The Lizards of October*, and how my life and career would have changed had he backed the book, he shook his head and told me, "It would have hurt you more than helped you. That novel was a piece of shit."

Had a rich La Jolla girlfriend. Gretchen. Oh: Gretchen! She was eighteen and drove a Porsche and liked slumming with me, "the poet." I still had my Jim Morrison complex then, my hair long, my clothes black, my attitude brooding and serious. She liked to read Bukowski. She was just as excited to see the poems he had sent me. And before I could accept his poems and write him back, I got another envelope from him. Ten poems! From Buk!

Thought of publishing them as a chapbook but a friend in Michigan, Kurt Nimmo, had gotten into trouble doing that—he too received a batch of poems from Bukowski and he created a chapbook out of them for his Planet Detroit Press, *Relentless as the Tarantula.* 500 copies. That's it. The owner of Black Sparrow Press, John Martin, somehow got wind of this and called Nimmo and threatened to sue him. Seems Martin had exclusive rights to Bukowski in any book form, even sixteen stapled pages. Nimmo was worried the thereat of legal action was real—Black Sparrow had the money for it, and he was some guy living in a single-wide trailer and using beer money to publish things. Martin called him back and made a deal: if my friend sent him every remaining copy of the chapbook, he could have any title on the Black Sparrow list in exchange, and there'd be no legal action. Nimmo took the deal. Man, I wish I still had my copy of that chap; it would fetch hundreds of dollars from collectors today, as it was signed. You can find an unsigned copy on eBay for around fifty dollars.

Bukowski's phone number was on the poetry manuscripts. Gretchen urged me to call him. I was too afraid. She said she would—that he'd probably respond better to a girl's voice.

She dialed. He answered. She said we wanted to publish his poems. He said, "Okay." I don't think he even remembered sending me anything. "Another fucking what?" he said. "Oh yeah, yeah," he said, "I like the title, yeah, I like the title."

Gretchen asked if we could come by some time and say hello. He hesitated. I'm sure people bothered him all the time—he wrote about it. He said, "Yeah, sure, why the hell not."

The next week, we drove to Los Angeles to meet my hero. I was so nervous I could barely speak. Gretchen had a fake I.D., so we bought a six-pack of Budweiser to give him, our offering to the God of plebian lit.

Expected him to live in a rundown, beat-up house. He resided in a very nice home, quite suburban. There was an old Volkswagen and a BMW in the driveway. His wife was in the backyard doing something. He was shorter than I expected, and had bad breath and dandruff. He thanked us for the beer, but said he was only drinking quality wine these days. "My stomach," he said. So Gretchen and I drank the beer and he drank water. He was a quiet man, a tired-looking man. His socks didn't seem to match. We sat in his living room with him.

"So you kids publish a little mag," he said.

"Yes," we said.

"Well," he said. He grinned. "Well."

Didn't know what to say. He kept looking at Gretchen's chest, neck, hair, and her legs—she was wearing a short skirt.

There was some chitchat. There were so many profound revelations I wanted to confess, and what his work meant to me, blah, blah, blah; but the reality was this: I was a seventeen-year-old kid, what the fuck did I know?

Gretchen mostly chatted—about La Jolla and the beaches and that Raymond Chandler once lived in La Jolla.

"You kids ever read John Fante?" he asked.

We hadn't.

"You should. Try him."

We nodded our heads.

"Well kids," he said, "I gotta get back to work."

He signed my copy of *Relentless as the Tarantula*, drawing a little old man figure with a wine bottle next to his signature.

We thanked him for his time and left.

He died ten years later.

Driving back to San Diego, Gretchen said she wanted to be a small press publisher with me. "You shouldn't do Buk's poems on a photocopy machine," she said. "*AFR* should be like a book, big, 300 pages, perfect bound."

"Sure, with what money?"

40

"Mine. I have an allowance. What would it cost?"

"$1,000?"

"No prob. Let's do it."

That never happened. I never got around to publishing Bukowski because there was never another issue of my zine. Gretchen and I went different ways five weeks later, and I lost interest in poetry and the small press.

4.

ELEMENTS OF DIRTY REALISM

ALCOHOL

Bukowski and Carver wrote a great deal about booze. Both were hospitalized for their drinking issues, both nearly died. Carver found AA and quit, Bukowski continued drinking—in his autumnal years he switched to expensive wine (which he could afford), as his stomach couldn't handle cheap beer and wine, or hard liquor, anymore. Carver, although he had stopped, reached into his past and wrote about being drunk and the problems of being drunk; these issues are the content of his finest stories.

Drinking in both their work is never fun, never much of a party, never social and harmless. Their narrators and characters drink because they are depressed, frightened, and lonely. Their drinking helps them to deal with the aesthetics of the ugly—poverty, forced to work menial jobs, being obscure and unknown writers, body issues, being intimate with the "wrong women." Booze is not an escape

THE DIRTY REALISM DUO

or a coping mechanism, it winds up causing more problems. In "Gazebo," Duane the narrator muses:

> Drinking's funny. When I look back on it, all of our important decisions have been figured out when we were drinking. Even when we talked about having to cut back on our drinking, we'd be sitting at the kitchen table or at our picnic table with a six-pack our whiskey (107).

In the poem "drink" from *Betting on the Muse*, Buk writes:

> I asked for a glass
> of wine.
> [...]
> There was the
> faint taste of
> turpentine. (87)

I could go on for hundreds of pages quoting Bukowski and drinking, but you get the picture, and you know that being a boozer is one of the endearing negative qualities that fans and critics have enjoyed about Buk.

CANCER

They died of cancer, six years apart, Carver first. Carver was fifty and Bukowski was seventy-four. When Bukowski was fifty his career was just getting on the fast track, going from obscure to international bestselling author. It is curious to think about what ray would have written had he lived to be seventy-four. Hell, fifty-four. Had he said all that he had to say about life in America, now that his own life was comfortable and there wasn't the

43

struggle? The sad irony is that just as he won the fights over poverty, alcohol, and literary obscurity, he could not relax and enjoy it—he had a new fight, the battle with lung cancer. Bukowski was battling leukemia, and he'd pretty much said all he had to say—his posthumous poetry is rehashing subjects and events he'd written a great deal about, and his last novel, *Pulp*, should never have been published in my opinion (it is dedicated to bad writing)—it was an awful attempt at the private eye genre, just as Richard Brautigan's gumshoe novel failed. And Paul Auster, writing as Paul Benjamin, hoping to make a quick buck. Some great authors simply cannot write genre, and some can—Graham Greene and Norman Mailer could switch to the private eye. 'Tis a pity, as they say (whoever *they* are), because the private detective novel is as American as literature can get.

WORK

Employment haunts Bukowski and Carver male characters. They seek it, they try to hang on, they get fired, they can't find it. In *Factotum* (meaning, "jack of all trades") Bukowski chronicles Chinaski's endless search for work—from warehouses to manual labor—to survive. The rent is always late and there is never enough money for booze. In *Post Office*, Chinaski holds two terms of employment for the U.S. Postal System, one as a carrier, the other as a clerk.

Carver's characters are always "in between jobs," unemployed and depressed. In "Vitamins," an out-of-work sales girl considers prostitution to make some much-needed quick money; in "Night School," a grown man is forced to move back in with his parents because he is un-employed and separated from his wife; the first line of "Collectors is "I was out of work" (122) and "They're Not Your Husband" starts off "Earl Ober was between jobs as a salesman" (22).

Work is a four-letter word in Dirty Realism—it is either loathed or not there, but it is a constant necessity.

WOMEN

Bukowski and Carver women are, much to the chagrin of feminists, easily categorized and pigeon-holed, often not in the best or progressive light. With Carver, they are either wives or ex-wives, girlfriends or ex-girlfriends, working as waitresses, secretaries, sales girls or star-at-home mothers. With Bukowski, they tend to be barflies, prostitutes, nymphomaniacs, or writers/poets looking for his sexual mentorship. Sometimes they are ex-wives and ex-girlfriends in Bukowski, but he does not write love stories. In Women, he goes from one encounter to another, but never truly falls in love. Carver writes a different kind of love story—his loves are futile and filled with despair; men love their women when there is a separation of divorce. In "Intimacy," a man doesn't realize how much he still loves his ex-wife until he sees her four years. In "Will You pleas Be Quiet, Please?" a man loves his wife so much that jealousy consumes him and his love turns ugly.

THE UGLY

And so that is what Dirty Realism is—discourse on the ugliness of modern life, poetry on the beauty of the human grotesque. Dirty Realism is telling the dirty truth—about unattractive people who get drunk, puke, fight, shit their pants, sleep with strangers, and do the wrong thing and suffer the consequences. Dirty Realism is about the everyday things most people would rather sugar coat or forget…. Carver and Bukowski remind us of these things, in all the repulsive—yet gorgeous—detail.

PART II

BUK

You have to have been in love to write poetry

---Raymond Carver,
            "You Don't Know What Love Is"

5.

THE LOS ANGELES NOVEL

"Los Angeles is 72 suburbs in search of a city."
   ---Dorothy Parker

John Fante, Charles Bukowski, and Dan Fante have written some of the most important contributions to what has become a sub-genre in its own right, "the Los Angeles novel." Bukowski decreed Fante as his greatest inspiration, more so than Knut Hamsun and Louis-Ferdinand Céline. During his youthful down and out days, Bukowski stumbled across *Ask the Dust* in the Los Angeles Public Library, where he spent time to escape the heat and trouble. "Like a man who found gold in a city dump," he recounts in the Foreword to the Black Sparrow Press edition,

> I carried the book to a table. The lines rolled calmly across the page, there was a flow. Each line had its own energy and was followed by another like it. The very substance of each line gave the page a form, a feeling of something

carved into it. And here, at last, was a man who was not afraid of emotion (p. 3).

Fante had published his first short story in *The American Mercury* in 1932, resulting in a lifelong epistle relationship with editor H. L. Mencken. Further fiction appeared in all the right literary places an up-and-coming writer needed to be: *The Atlantic Monthly*, *The Saturday Evening Post*, *Collier's*, *Esquire*, and *Harper's Bazaar*. His first novel, *Wait Until Spring, Bandini*, was released in 1938. His second, *Ask the Dust*, was a bestseller. He was wooed by Hollywood and the better paychecks screenwriting provided, his credits including *The Reluctant Saint* and *Walk on the Wild Side*. Fante vanished into obscurity around the same time Bukowski had discovered him, who, according to Stephen Cooper in *Full of Life*, lived

> in a rented room in downtown Los Angeles where he was trying to become a writer, drinking to excess, starving and in general driving himself if not strictly mad then ever further from accommodation with convention, literary or otherwise. Before winding up in the charity ward of County General Hospital in the mid-1950s hemorrhaging from a bleeding ulcer, Bukowski had published only one short story, "Aftermath of a Lengthy Rejection Slip" had appeared in the March-April 1944 issue of *Story* when Bukowski was twenty-four years old, a conscious homage to the two writers who had influenced him, Knut Hamsun and even more so John Fante (pp. 307-308).

If there hadn't been a John Fante, there may have not been a Charles Bukowski; and if there had not been a Bukowski, there would not have been a second life for Fante. Other than Robert Towne's options on the out-of-print and forgotten *Ask the Dust* and *The Brotherhood of the Grape*, contemporary readers had no idea who Fante was. In *Women*, Bukowski's alter ego, Henry Chinaski, states that Fante is his favorite writer; on the dedication page of *Love Is a Dog from Hell: Poems 1974-1977*, Bukowski writes, "For John Fante—who taught me how." Fante, however, had never read or heard of Bukowski. Although Bukowski knew his hero lived in the L.A. area, he had never met him and "out of respect for his idol, [he] never dared approach Fante" (*Full of Life* 309). Black Sparrow Press publisher John Martin asked who Fante was—a question during a telephone conversation that would be life altering for Fante and prove to be a significant mark in contemporary American fiction. Martin read *Ask the Dust*, reprinted it, and Arturo Bandini was back from oblivion, forty years later. Critics lauded Fante the rediscovery of the decade, and readers were buying enough copies to allot much needed financial security for the ailing, now blind writer. Black Sparrow reissued his other out-of-print novels and published his dusty manuscripts, as well as a new one, *Dreams from Bunker Hill*, in 1983, composed via dictation, the final volume in the Bandini cycle. A year later, he died at the age seventy-four.

Dan Fante, following his father's mighty boot steps, dedicates some of his work to the man who brought him into this world and set him on the course of the literary life. He wrote a play, *Don Giovanni*, based on his father's last years and coming to term with his two sons. "When I was a kid," he tells the *Lummox Journal*, "my old man was a failed novelist and screenwriter [...] honestly, he was a fix-it journeyman hack screenwriter, forget novelist. He was unfamous." He dedicates *Short Dog* to his father: "Thank you! You magnificent sonofabitch!" (7) "He wasn't the great John Fante when I was [...] a kid or a young man or an adult," he tells in Rob Woodward in an interview,

> until I was in my late thirties/early forties he wasn't anything. He was just a cynical, angry old screenwriter. You couldn't come near him because he'd cut you off at the knees if you said the wrong thing to him. His sensibility toward literature, toward writing, was what filtered, was what impacted me, his judgment of literature and his extreme sensitivity and passion [...]You live with somebody like that and you can't help but assimilate his headspace; it can't help but rub off on you.

Fante has been compared more to Bukowski than his father for scenes of excessive drinking and wayward sexual adventures. But he was not influenced by Bukowski; he cites Herbert Selby, Jr. for that role. As for Bukowski, he tells Woodward:

> His stuff in very uneven [...] people confuse stylistic element with content. Bukowski wrote the way he did because he had to — but his content, that's the important part. People don't understand his subtlety and they just think if you write about people puking in their beds and

having sex with hookers and vomiting that you've made it—and there's so much more to it. Because it's the novel that's the important thing, the content; it's the feelings conveyed in the novel.

Chump Change was first published in France, and his collection of cab driver stories, *Short Dog*, in England, before they were picked up by the independent Sun Dog Press in Michigan. His play, *Boiler Room*, enjoyed a fourteen-month run on Los Angeles' theater row; about telemarketers, it was compared to David Mamet's *Glen Glarry Glen Ross*. His fiction slowly reaped respect and critical attention; for his second novel, *Mooch*, he signed with Canongate Books.

Although published as fiction, the works of these three men are autobiographical in nature, told in the first person, each narrator possessing names close to the respective writer: Arturo Bandini, Henry Chinaski[5], and Bruno Dante. The alter-egos are also struggling writers (later, for Chinaski, in *Women* and *Hollywood*, he writes of being a famous one), describing the joys and sorrow, the hardships and process, of trying to survive, write, and get published in Los Angeles.

---

[5] Bukowski's first name is actually Henry, middle name Charles. He started using his middle name because his father (Hank Bukowski senior) showed copies of the magazines he published in to co-workers and friends, claiming he was the author. In *Ham on Rye*, he tells how the father throws the son out of the house after reading the son's manuscripts.

Bandini, for instance, has published a few short stories in *Ask the Dust*, preparing himself to compose a novel—and nothing less the elusive Great American Novel. In *Post Office*, Chinaski is working for the federal government, delivering mail, while writing poetry and publishing in the small press. In *Chump Change*, Bruno Dante has returned to Los Angeles because his father is on his deathbed; he works on short stories when he's sober enough to think. Los Angeles plays an important part of the landscape of these novels—Bandini is living on Bunker Hill (now downtown Los Angeles), Chinaski is delivering mail to Angelenos, and Dante does not want to be back home yet winds up staying longer than he anticipated, doing what he can to survive in the City of Angels—usually telemarketing or signing lonely women up for a dating service (he excels at both). Fante, Bukowski, and Fante are not only writing about their lives and reflections, they are writing about, and addressing, the city of Los Angeles—they are reacting to the city, and the city reacts back: it is a relationship.

Fante's first novel, *Wait Until Spring, Bandini*, is written in third person, and the other Bandini novels are in the first. It is a coming-of-age story; Bandini is a child, similar to *Ham on Rye*, where Henry Chinaski is also a boy experiencing the painful wonders of the world. "Arturo Bandini was pretty sure he wouldn't go to hell when he died" (*Fante Reader* 52) and Chinaski remembers "my grandmother saying [...] 'I will bury *all* of you!'" (*Ham on Rye* 10). Dan Fante has not written a novel about the childhood of Bruno. *The Road to Los Angeles* is the second in the Bandini chronicles and was not published until 1985. It is a glib yarn. In 1936, Knopf and Vanguard Press were seriously considering publishing it, but ultimately, according to Cooper, rejected the manuscript as "unworthy of publication" and yet "extremely provocative" (133). Knopf did so with "particularly great disappointment" (133) since Fante had made an impression on the literary world with his short stories. After several more rejections, Fante put the book away. In it, Bandini's father is dead; he is the man of the house, cohabitating with his mother and sister "in an apartment house next door to a place where a lot of Filipinos lived" (16). Bandini is writing, but not publishing, his "head swims to transvaluated phantasmagoria of phrases" (99). He lists his employment record in the Los Angeles Harbor.

> My first job was ditchdigging a short time after I graduated high school. Every night I couldn't sleep from the pain in my back. We were digging an excavation in an empty lot, there wasn't any shade, the sun came straight from a cloudless sky, and I was down in that hole digging with two huskies who dug with the love for it, always laughing and telling jokes, laughing and smoking bitter tobacco (9).

He quits the backbreaking labor and becomes a dishwasher for a month, then a "flunkie" on a truck. "All we did was move boxes of toilet tissue from the warehouse to the harbor grocery stores in San Pedro and Wilmington" (10). Next he becomes a grocery clerk, until he is caught pilfering a ten dollar bill from the till. Through all this he is reading books, such as Nietzsche's *Man and Superman*, preparing for the writer's life. His family is not supportive, however—his mother believes literature is an impractical waste of time, his sister reads his novel manuscript and finds it "strange; very strange indeed" (147). His co-workers joke about his aspirations, telling him that he writes about "puke." Working at a fishing cannery like some forgotten Steinbeck character, Bandini knows he has to get away from his family and strike out on his own. He composes a letter:

> Dear Woman Who Gave Me Life:
>
> The callous vexations and perturbations of this night have subsequently resolved themselves to a state which precipitates me, Arturo Bandini, into brobdingagian and gargantuan decision. I inform you of this in no uncertain terms. Ergo, I now leave you and your ever charming daughter [...] and seek the fabulous usufructs of my incipient career in profound solitude (p. 163).

In *Ask the Dust*, Bandini arrives to L.A. a minor published writer with plans for Greatness with a capital G. He falls in love with a Mexican waitress who has her own dreams of greatness, which does not include being with a poor gringo short story writer. In *Dreams from Bunker Hills*, he has published more but is still struggling:

> My first collision with fame was hardly memorable. I was a busboy at Max's Deli. The year was 1934. The place was Third and Hill, Los Angeles. I was twenty-one years old [...] I was a busboy nonpareil, with great verve and style for the profession, and though I was dreadfully underpaid (one dollar a day plus meals) I attracted considerable attention as I whirled

from table to table [...] This phenomenon became
known one day after a drunken photographer from
the Los Angeles Times sat at the bar, snapped several
pictures of me serving a customer as she looked up at
me with admiring eyes. Next day there was a feature
story attached to the Times photograph. It told of the
struggle and success of young Arturo Bandini, an
ambitious, hard-working kid from Colorado, who had
crashed through the difficult magazine world with the
sale of his first story to *The American Phoenix* (p. 3).

Henry Chinaski is in the same Los Angeles predica-
ment—a published writer who has to work menial jobs.
Employment with the United State Postal Service "began
as a mistake," *Post Office* starts.[6] "It was Christmas sea-
son and I learned from the drunk up the hill, who did the
trick every Christmas, that they would damn near hire
anybody, and so I went and the next thing I knew I had
this leather sack on my back and I was hiking around at
my leisure" (13). He enters the secret, strange world of
mail couriers, where "each day it was another goddamned
thing, and you were always ready for rape, murder, dogs,

---

[6] The story behind the writing and publishing of *Post Office* is the stuff of
literary legend. John Martin, a local business owner turned publisher,
offered to support Bukowski for the rest of his life is he quit his postal
clerk job and wrote full time. It was 1969 and the agreed upon monthly
stipend was $100, a sum Bukowski determined was adequate to pay
rent and pay for food, booze, and horse race betting. Different economic times indeed! In a letter to friend Barry Miles, he writes: "I have
one of two choices—stay in the post office and go crazy...or stay out
here and play at writer and starve. I have decided to starve." Bukowski
would claim to write *Post Office* in three weeks. Martin published it via
Black Sparrow Press in 1971. That turned out to be an intelligent business move on Martin's part, as Bukowski's books would eventually
make both men quite financially secure.

or insanity of some sort" (21). His descriptions of the employment are criminal, admitting to drinking on the job and stealing money out of birthday cards. He works as a carrier for three years and then happily resigns. "Little did I know that in a couple of years I would be back as a clerk," he confessed, "and that I would clerk, all hunched-up on a stool, for nearly 12 years" (50).[7] *Post Office* has all the elements of his other novels, and what his work, in general, is best known for: wild drinking bouts, hectic relationships with alcoholic women, writing poetry on napkins and grocery bags, and betting on the horse races, all elements of what has been deemed (along with the stories of Raymond Carver) "Dirty Realism."[8]

> I had a run of luck at the racetrack. I began to
> feel confident out there. You went for a certain
> profit each day, somewhere between fifteen and
> forty bucks. You didn't too much. If you didn't

---

[7] Bill Buford, in his editorial for the theme issue of *Granta* on Dirty Realism, states that the sub-genre is "not a fiction devoted to making the large historical statement [...]a fiction of a difference scope – devoted to the local details, the nuances, the little disturbances in language and gesture [...] unadorned, unfurnished, low-rent tragedies about people who watch day-time television, read cheap romances or listen to country and western music. They are waitresses in roadside cafes, cashiers in supermarkets, construction workers, secretaries and unemployed cowboys. They play bingo, eat cheeseburgers, hunt deer and stay in cheap hotels. They drink a lot and are often in trouble: for stealing a car, breaking a window, pickpocketing a wallet [...] drifters in a world cluttered with junk food and the oppressive details of modern consumerism [...] the belly-side of contemporary life (4).

[8] Bukowski was nearly fired when his superiors got wind of his weekly column in the *Open City* and the *Los Angeles Free Press*, later collected in *Notes of a Dirty Old Man*, because he wrote about his work as a postal clerk, none of it flattering to the USPS.

hit early, you bet a little more, enough so that if the horse came in, you had your profit margin. I kept coming back, day after day (p. 53).

Factotum is his most popular title with fans, and was recently made into an independent movie starring Matt Dillon as the young, wandering, writing, drinking Chinaski. *Factotum* follows Bukowski from L.A., New Orleans, and back to L.A., going from job to job, woman to woman, destitute and lost. By the time of *Women*, Chinaski is neither poor nor lost—he is a famous writer now, with female fans sending him naked pictures in the mail; some of them he invites to come to L.A. and visit for sex. These encounters he reveals in funny, sad, and desperate detail; while many critics have labeled him chauvinistic, Russell Harrison, in *Against the American Dream*, contends that in *Women*, "there was an increased subtlety of characterization, a more nuanced treatment of psychological dynamics and less reliance on stereotypes" (183). He is "constantly horny" (77) and enjoying the benefits of literary fame, either at home or while traveling the country and giving readings at universities. There is definitely a long list of conquests in the book, many about a man his fifties sleeping with women half his age. These women want to fall in love with the man whose writing they are in love with, only to discover the actual writer is not the man they envisioned.

…she frightened me. I couldn't understand what she was doing there with me. She didn't appear to be a groupie. I went to the bathroom, came back and turned out the light. I could feel her getting into bed next to me. I took her in my arms and we began kissing. I couldn't believe my luck. What right had I? How could a few books of poems call this forth? (p. 90)

Women, anthropologically, paints a time capsule of the underground literary scene of Los Angeles in the 1970s, filled with angry, competitive poets and maverick small magazine publishers. "Writers came by, all of them poets," he writes in *The Captain is Out to Lunch and the Sailors Have Taken Over the Ship.*

POETS. And I discovered a curious thing: none of them had any visible means of support. If they had books out they didn't sell. And if they gave poetry readings, few attended, say from 4 to 14 other POETS. But they all live din fairly nice apartments and seemed to have plenty of time to sit on my couch and drink my beer. I had gotten the reputation in town of being the wild one, of having parties where untold things happened and crazy women danced and broke things, or I threw people off my porch or there were police raids or etc. and etc. Much of this was true. But I also had to get the word down for my publisher and for the magazines to get the rent and the booze money, and this meant writing prose (p. 85).

The Chinaski in *Hollywood,* however, is older, richer, married, living in a suburban house, and tackling Tinsel Town by way of a French director. Norman Mailer makes a cameo. The Los Angeles in his previous novels is not the same city—he is no longer as scared, as drunk (having switched to quality wine for health reasons), or in need of employment.

Work. Bukowski's early fiction and poetry, and John Fante's overall writing, is chiefly concerned with looking for a job, keeping a job, making money to eat, pay rent, exist. "No contemporary American novelist has treated works as extensively or intensively as Bukowski," Harrison notes (123). Labor in Los Angeles is also prevalent with Bruno Dante. In *Chump Change*, Dante has recently been released from twenty-eight days in rehabilitation; he travels with his wife to Los Angeles because his father, Jonathan Dante, author and screenwriter, is in the hospital, dying. He does not care for being back home and the bad memories he has of growing up in southern California. He takes off with the car and his father's dog, leaving his wife with his family, and proceeds to go on a long drinking binge, living in a motel with a skinny underage meth-addicted prostitute he purchased for fifty dollars. "L.A.'s weather in December is particularly nuts," he muses. "The last few years, at Christmas time, people drive to the canyons to start fires hoping to burn the city down and see the disaster they've caused reported on the TV news that night" (77).

In *Mooch*, Dante is sober, in A.A., still in Los Angeles, and working the telemarketing racket. "I hated being back in L.A.," he admits. "I hated that I hadn't a drink in months" (1). The novel chronicles Dante's struggle with staying away from alcohol and drugs, his falling off the wagon, going back to rehab, and his getting involved with the wrong women and the wrong jobs, betraying those who try to help him recover. Although a collection, *Short Dog: Cab Driver Stories from the L.A. Streets* read like a novel in related stories, concerning Dante's experiences as a hack and "a fellow Los Angeles-based would-be writer wandering a purgatory of dehumanizing labor and self-obstructing vices" (Wranovics).[6] The first entry, "Wife-beater Bob," shows Dante learning the ropes, and politics, of being a cabbie, while the last, "1647 Ocean Front Walk," describes the event that, "after that day, I never drove a taxi again" (114). A passenger in his cab—a bereaved, insane rich woman—after the death of her elderly mother, jumps out a high rise window, taking her twenty-year-old daughter with her. There's the possibility that he could have done something to stop the suicide/murder, as the woman left him a cryptic message on his machine. In "Marble Man," Dante takes a break from driving and goes back to the phones, "slamming unsuspecting mooches" (45), and gets into a compromising sexual situation with his boss' young, Beverly Hills-bred wife.

The difference in these three writers is that John Fante is always hopeful for the future, Bukowski finds the black humor in every depressing situation, and Dan Fante is bleak and hopeless. Bandini, at all times, maintains integrity to his path and ideals; Chinaski is just trying to get by and means nobody harm; and Dante, without a care, hurts people, lets them down, and is not a reliable character: "Everything I touched seemed to be turning to pain" (*Short Dog* 23) he concludes, and then kills his girlfriend's new dog out of jealousy. Still, Dan Fante reaches a gritty, flirty realism—beyond dirty—a true and ugly poetry of the street, soaked eighty proof and suicidal, that neither his father nor Bukowski have come close to when writing about hopelessness and pain. There is always a sense of, no matter how bad things are, Bukowski's Chinaski is going to be okay the next day, and Fante's Bandini will always survive on his wits—but Bruno Dante, who knows what the next drinking binge will bring, as he attempts to kill himself in *Mooch* and is constantly in and out of violent trouble, going off on "three-day drunken binges, blackouts and seamy assignations fueled by the better-known fortified wines (Night Train, Ripple, Thunderbird) and whatever else chance puts within easy grasp," writes Wranovics.

> But unlike prototypical Los Angeles tough guys like Raymond Chandler's idealistic private eye Philip Marlowe, the flawed Bruno Dante traverses Los Angeles's mean streets only to confront the corruption and degeneracy within himself. The landmarks on this tour are Cedars-Sinai, the East Hollywood Alcohol and Drug Relief Program, the Metropolitan Center for Hypnotherapy and Brotmann's Hospital, way stations where the walking wounded get patched up or pretend their way through rehab.

There is a glimmer of hope for Dante at the end of *Chump Change*, though. "In a few hours it would be midnight and I would have gone a full day on my own without a drink," he states at the end of the book. "If I stayed off the booze, I knew I'd be able to write again" (198).

Every major American city—an entity with its own personality—has its definitive novels: New York, Chicago, Pittsburgh, and San Francisco have plenty. I am leaving out many obvious works, that topic is for a book-length study—from Nathaniel West to Raymond Chandler, Kate Braverman, Steve Erickson, Elmore Leonard, and Bret Easton Ellis, the list is long. Epic movies have been made: *Sunset Boulevard*, *Day of the Locust*, *Grand Canyon*, *Magnolia*, *Short Cuts*, and *Crash*; in the mix has been Bukowski's *Barfly* and Fante's *Ask the Dust*. All these works reveal a Los Angeles as seen by their creators, the city always done anew. Fante's Los Angeles is just beginning, a city where a young man can become famous and find love; Bukowski's is a challenge, a slouching beast to fight against, a smoggy Grendel to battle and win; Fante's is a whore, used up, compromised, vilified, and victimized. It is "real, vivid, science fiction" (*Chump Change* 20), "cloudless, flawless" (*Short Dog* 101) and "burning, suffocating" (*Mooch* 1). "I don't know if we could define the L.A. writer because nobody is from L.A.," Dan Fante argues to Woodward.

> They all come here and are all cynicized by this vacuous dream that is Los Angeles. We are all consumed by smog and heat and freeway shootings [...] people from the Midwest or from the east are influenced; they think about Bukowski living in east Hollywood in a busted out apartment and drinking Budweiser, and my father...

Likewise, the young Bukowski "often walked past the rooming house where he imagined Fante lived in the days of his early struggle," according to Harrison, "fantasizing that he, Charles Bukowski, was Arturo Bandini, self-proclaimed greatest writer who ever lived" (308).

"It's poor, struggling, and passionate that I think qualifies the L.A. writer," Dan Fante says.

The same can be said for the Los Angeles novel.

6.

SUICIDE NOTES ON A PROPOSAL FOR A BOOK CALLED

CHARLES BUKOWSKI: AUTOBIOGRAPHY AND PERFORMANCE ETHNOGRAPHY IN HIS POETRY AND PROSE

NOTE: The following is a proposal for the original idea of this study. I sent it to a few academic publishers but no one took a bite. Looking it over, I thought, why the book when all the points I want to get across about Bukowski's writing are addressed in this document?

OVERVIEW

This critical study closely examines the use of autobiography and the memoir in Charles Bukowski's body of work: poetry, "fiction," newspaper columns, journal writing, and published letters. Bukowski, a popular writer of the 1970s-'90s, and still so today, was known to have fully exercised his demons in his confessional poetry and prose, writing about alcoholism, sex, gambling, and dealing with the fame that came to him late in his life, when he went from a destitute, unknown underground writer to an international bestselling author, hounded by the press and fans. He chronicled his entire journey in his writings, the majority of which were unapologetically autobiographical. His honesty of the seedier side of life, being down and out, being desperate, being confused about fame, was what drew loyal readers to his work. The few times he delved into actual fiction (a private eye novel and two collections of stories) proved to be works that were not well received and not as appreciated by critics and fans. Some critics felt he was too autobiographical, he revealed too much, and was repetitive, hashing out events in his life both in poetry and prose. In the late 1970s, he and Raymond Carver were categorized as writers of "dirty realism," by exploring autobiographical topics that respectable writers shied away from—both he and Carver were ostracized by the academics of literature for exploiting their personal relationships and personal issues with alcohol, drugs, and sex. Finally, Bukowski is also dubbed a "California writer," as most of his work is set in Los Angeles: his work acts as ethnography, revealing blue collar, low-income life and conditions in Los Angeles in the 1970s and 1980s, and the sub-culture of small press poetry writers and publishing, which is an anthropological study all of its own.

THE IMPORTANCE OF THIS BOOK

Bukowski studies are on the rise. In the last five years, a number of critical works have been published, when before there were few—Twayne's study is the best of them.

In 2005, three were issued, but are more biographies and reflections by people who knew him. The published studies on Bukowski tend to look at a broad range of disciplines: political, sociological, and economical, as he wrote about the working class poor. This study solely focuses on his use, and technique, of memoir in the form of poetry, prose, columns, journals, and letters.

CHAPTERS OUTLINE

Chapter One: Poetry

Close examination of Bukowski's use of poetry as memoir. His poetry, for the most part, was prosaic, narrative, and confessional: whether funny, dramatic, or traumatic, Bukowski reflected on his life experiences in this form. He was quite prolific, and like any prolific writer, often repeated himself, or examined the same events and experiences in several works—so what new insights did he arrive at when returning to something he already wrote about? This chapter covers the collections of poetry published when he was alive, and the numerous posthumous books, which are still being published. What new things are learned about a dead writer from work that possibly should not see print? (Many of his post-death collections are sub-standard in quality, or simply repeat already published work.)

Chapter Two: Novels

Bukowski did not publish fictional novels. All his novels, except one, were memoir. He always wrote in the first person, his narrator is "Henry Chinaski." Henry is Bukowski's real first name, Charles his middle. His first "novel" was *Post Office*, chronicling the twelve years he worked for the U.S. Post Office, and his last was *Hollywood*, chronicling his experiences in the movie business and the making of the film, *Barfly*. *Ham on Rye* is about his childhood, and *Women* is about his dealing with fame, money, and success. None of these books were ever published, as "fiction" but "literature" and some bookstores will shelve them in non-fiction and autobiography sections.

Chapter Three: Life in the Columns

Part of what made Bukowski's name known, going from an obscure poet to an international sensation, was his personal columns in *Open City* and the *Los Angeles Free Press*, alternative southern Californian newspapers. His column was called "Notes of a Dirty Old Man," which City Lights Press collected in a book of the same name. He was not restricted or censored by his editors and wrote openly and honestly about true events in his life, which caused many of his readers to show up at his door, wishing to experience his wild life of excessive drinking and madness with him. This chapter also reflects on the use of the newspaper column as a form of memoir, practiced by hundreds of writers today.

Chapter Four: The Computer and the Journal

When Bukowski, late in his career, bought a Macintosh computer in the early 1990s, taking a class to figure out how to use it, he began to keep a journal. He was now wealthy, famous, living in a large house, drinking expensive wine instead of cheap beer and wine...his wild days were over, he was married and the experiences he was known for were behind him. In his journals, he reflected on his past, as he had nothing new to write about. These journals were serialized in some literary magazines and collected in two books published by Black Sparrow Press.

Chapter Five: Letters

This chapter examines the published letters that have recently been collected in four volumes, and what further insights Bukowski revealed about his life in them. In some ways, his letters were the same as his poetry and prose: honest and to the point, a man reflecting on his personal experiences. Published letters, in chronological form, often create a de facto memoir.

Chapter Six: Films

This chapter examines the two movies made about Bukowski's life: *Barfly*, that he wrote himself, based on several works, and *Factotum*, based on the novel with the same title. How well does autobiography translate into film, and what is its purpose? What draws viewers to such films, especially with Bukowski's life?

Chapter Seven: Influences

This chapter takes a look at the autobiographical writers that most influenced Bukowski: John Fante, Knut Hamsun, Henry Miller, and Ferdinand Céline. Like him, these four writers never wrote "fiction," but life writing in the form of the "novel." Hamsun and Céline, both modernist European writers, wrote in forms very unlike American literature; however, Bukowski's writings resembled John Fante's the most. Fante was another California writer, his books all set in Los Angeles. This chapter also discusses Bukowski's influence on others, individual writers or a movement: when he started to become famous, dozens of poetry and prose writers began to imitate him, which gave life to the term "Bukowski-esque." More writers started to turn to the form of straight autobiography, rather than fiction or abstract poetry. Did Bukowski have a hand in today's popularity of life writings? Finally, there have been a number of recent memoirs written by people who knew him, writing about their personal experiences with Bukowski—this chapter examines those books.

Chapter Eight: Auto/ethnography

In anthropology and sociology, a new form of writing has come into its own, called "auto/ethnography." This is when the researcher becomes reflexive—while studying other people, the ethnographer turns inward and studies himself: his past, his experiences, his interpretation of reality. As a California writer, reporting on a time, place, and American culture, Bukowski's work operates as ethnography, as well as auto/ethnography. This chapter considers the theories of auto/ethnography and how Bukowski fits within it.

7.

GUILT & GRACE:
HOW CHARLES BUKOWSKI INTERPRETED
HIS FAME & FORTUNE

A REFLEXIVE CRITICAL ESSAY PRESENTED WITH BROKEN LINES
TO LOOK LIKE A POEM IN THE BUKOWSKI STYLE

....a few years or decades from now, I will think nothing about
everything.
> ---William T. Vollmann, *Rising Up & Rising Down*

1. HOLLYWOOD & WESTERN:
A WEIRD COINCIDENCE

J.   a writer & actress,
    moved to Los Angeles a year ago.
    she's a Bukowski fan,
    to the point of obsession—a lot of women are.
the singer/songwriter Jewel
has publicly claimed Bukowski
is her favorite
poet & an influence,

although she spells
his name wrong
in her own volume
of verse,[9]
A Night Without Armour.

Sean Penn says he's
a big Bukowski fan,
interviewed him in
Interview magazine
& appeared in
the documentary
Born Into This.

Michael Madsen published
a book of bad Buk imitation
poems, *Burning in Paradise,*
although a few of them were
pretty good and heartfelt,
such as "Goodbye" that opens
with a confession:

---

[9] Audrey M. Clark, reviewing the book, says, "The poems in Jewel's collection consist of three subjects: love, childhood and observations about popular culture. Citing influences by Neruda, Dylan Thomas, Bukowski and Rumi, Jewel changes attitudes throughout the book almost as if she is changing clothes or hairstyles. For example, the first poem in the collection, "As a Child I Walked," is a simple poem based on the Romantic notion of God existing in nature, while the next poem, "The Bony Ribs of Adam," tries to compare choosing fame (as a performer) over love to the biblical story of Adam and Eve choosing personal desire over instructions from God. The narrator's attitudes shift so abruptly between these two poems that the reader is left wondering if there was some point s/he missed."

The first time I had sex
with a woman
I was 13 years old.
Her name was Jackie.
She said she was 28.
It wasn't only me
she fucked but
all my friends too.
  (p. 17)

Kind of like
the catch-phrase
in *Barfly*:
"Here's to all my friends!"

& so
it goes…

J. was
also 13,
like Madsen,
when
Bukowski died
of leukemia.
(she is 28 now,
like Jackie.)
she may have
been reading
him then.
she shared a shelf
of Bukowski titles
with her

ex-boyfriend in San Diego,
the musician who was
afraid to move to L.A.
w/her.
she found an apartment
on Carlton Way,
off Hollywood & Western,
& later learned that
her grandfather
once owned & operated
a taco shop @ the
infamous corner,
before there was
a red line
subway station
built underground.

"i think this means something,"
J. said,
"this has to *mean something*."

"maybe your grandfather's
soul guided you there,"
i said.

while taking
the red trolley
blue line
down to the U.S./Mexico
border
for my weekly visit
to Tijuana

to pick
up
cheap pharmaceuticals
& get a lap dance or blowjob
in the red light district
known as *zona norte*,
i was reading
Love Is a Dog from Hell (1977)
for my research
into a monograph
i was writing,
The Dirty Realism Duo:
Charles Bukowski
&
Raymond Carver
on the Aesthetics
of the Ugly[10]
& noticed several
mentions of
Hollywood & Western.
i called j. on her
blackberry
from my old,
clunky cell phone
& asked her if she'd
read this Buk
collection,
if she knew about
the references to
Hollywood & Western.

---

[10] The Borgo Press, 2008.

"i read it before," she said,
"but I don't have it,
it was tim's copy
& he has it—
i *wish* I had a
copy of that book."

she didn't remember
the reference but said
Buk had a poem that
mentioned a
liquor store
on Hollywood
& Normandie,
a few blocks from her apartment
& near
the stripper bar
i like to spend
quality time in.[11]

after i took care
of business in Tijuana[12]

---

[11] See www.jumbos.com.

[12] I became hooked on a certain pharmaceutical purchased over-the-counter in Tijuana called Tramadol. It was the last thing I expected: becoming, for want of a better, sugarcoated term, *a junkie*. I was addicted and didn't know how that happened. It was certainly never my intention and I didn't think it could be possible. These things just creep on you and then you're trapped in your need and you don't know what to do, you don't know where to turn, except inside: where you re-examine your life and find out where it all began, and try to come up with a means of bringing it to an end, short of checking into rehab like

THE DIRTY REALISM DUO

i returned home
& checked
one of the many Bukowski websites:
www.bukowski.net
that has been the

---

a celebutante with bad press. According to Wikipedia.org (I know, not a reliable source for citations), the drug is "an atypical opioid which is a centrally acting analgesic, used for treating moderate to severe pain. It is a synthetic agent, as a 4-phenyl-piperidine analogue of Codeine, and appears to have actions on the Gabaergic, noradrenergic and serotonergic systems. Tramadol was developed by the German pharmaceutical company Grünenthal GmbH and marketed under the trade name Tramal. Grünenthal has also cross-licensed the drug to many other pharmaceutical companies that market it under various names like Ultram, Ultracet, and Tramacet. Dosages vary depending on the degree of pain experienced by the patient."

When I initially checked Drugs.com, my understanding concluded Tramadol was not habit-forming; it wasn't narcotics-based like Vicodin or Oxycotin.

The first bottle I purchased was manufactured from a Mexican company called Venadrol; the bottle contained fifty pills and cost $18 at a pharmacy on Third and Revolucíon, next to the Burger King. I had walked in to procure Metaformin, a drug for those with Type II diabetes that assists the pancreas in correctly processing sugar into the bloodstream. In Tijuana, Metaformin was $10 for a bottle of 100, compared to a $25 co-pay at Keiser Permanente, $60 without insurance.

I asked the pharmacist if they had Vicodin. He shook his head and said, "Not without a prescription." I thought a prescription wasn't needed—this was *Tijuana*, after all, and street barkers sold Vicodin and Oxycotin for $5-10 a pill, along with meth, coke, and ecstasy. (I later learned that to get a prescription for almost anything, certain doctors would write one out for a fee of $25.)

"We have muscle relaxants," the pharmacist told me. "If you need a pain stopper, these do the same job."

"Yeah?"

"Take two or three, it is like one Vicodin," he said.

best research tools
for my critical study.
there are scans
of many
original manuscripts,
a searchable database,
& a timeline
that includes
past addresses of
Buk's homes.

there were
several addresses
on the eastern side
of Los Angeles,
& one downtown,
in the 1960s-70s.
there were two
on Carlton
Way:
5526 for a short while
& then 5327 2/5
from 1975 to 1978.

from there he
bought his house in
San Pedro where he
lived & wrote until is
death in 1994.

J. lives two buildings
away from his old

home on
Carton Way.

i was excited
to tell her this.

i sent her a
text message.

(Bukowski didn't
stick around to
see a world with
text messages
& Instant Messages,

google, AOL,
& YouTube.

he barely knew how to
operate his
Macintosh!)

j. was flabbergasted
when she got
the news.

"no wonder i like
that neighborhood so
much," i said.
"it's buk country."

"weird," she said.

"this must mean something,"
i said,
"it has to *mean something*."

"freaky," j. said.
"driving home,
i thought about writing
a poem about
this."

i gave her a title:

"Smeared Menstrual Blood
on the Same Sidewalk Bukowski
Puked Many Times On."

2. THREE PIVOTAL, TRANSITIONAL YEARS

those three years
on Carlton Way were
important, transitional
years.
Bukowski was writing
full-time, funded by
John Martin and
Black Sparrow Press.
he wrote *Factotum*
& *Women*
at that address,
plus many poems,
of course,

always the poems.

   as the poems increase into thousands you
   realize that you've created very
   little.

&

   the best writers have said very
   little

                         (*Betting On the Muse*, 211)

what makes
that address important
to Bukowski scholars
is that it is the space
where he parked
his wrinkled old ass
& wrote & wrote &
went from obscure poet—
or at least local cult writer—
to international
bestselling author,
now recognized as an
important contributor
to 20th century American
literature.

it is an unassuming
little street, tucked away two
blocks from
Hollywood & western,
near a giant empty

lot filled with trash &
the remnants of homeless
folk sleeping there
overnight.
most of the structures
are apartment buildings
& duplexes.
Bukowski was in a duplex,
the address suffix
2/5
is a giveaway.
they don't make addresses
like that anymore,
not in soCal.

many of the residents
are single people in their
20s-30s, going to school
or trying to make it
in one of the Los Angeles
big time career venues—
acting, filmmaking, music,
maybe even writing.

many more are Mexican
families,
living 4-15 in a single
apartment, many
probably illegal
& from guatemala
or el salvador,
playing their

loud BOOM BOOM
music long
into the night,
cheering, laughing,
slugging down many
cervezas & getting
drunk,
obnoxious,
bothering their white neighbors
& threatening them
w/guns or knives if
they complain,
these lousy gringos
who like to eat
tacos & drink Dos Equis
& pretend it is
a true culinary
ethnic
experience.

i wonder how many writers
are living
on Carlton Way
right now.
i wonder how many of
them know Bukowski
used to live
there three decades ago.
i wonder how many of
them even know who
Bukowski *is*.
most people

do *now*—he is a household
name, if someone hasn't
read him, they
have *heard*
of the name

(one time
my landlord gave me burnt CDs
of Bukowski's readings when
he read an article of
mine in the local weekly
& I mentioned Buk.)

i wonder who lives
in that space today.
i am afraid to knock,

i am afraid to ask.

i want to live there,
like room 31
@ the alta cienega motel
@ Hollywood & La
Cienega,
where Jim Morrison
resided off & on
in his pivotal years,
& now an important
room to stay in
for young musicians
& singers,
even famous ones

who want to absorb
the vibe of
the past,
to touch
the walls
he touched,
to have sex on
the bed
he may have had
sex on,
w/ all those
groupies who would
come to see
the lizard king

*who could
do anything,
yeah.*

3. FAME & FORTUNE

for most of the 1990s,
after *Barfly*,
& work published
after his death,
Bukowski focused
on the change in his
life, that he had money
now, that he was comfortable,
rich, not struggling
& down and out.

he lost many friends,
if they were really friends,
acquaintances & colleagues
in the small press
who were vehemently
jealous—

Chinaski only lets movie stars visit him
now, a poet wrote recently,
and while it's true that I might not have been
eager for a visit from *him*

("I am a Mole," *Slouching
Toward Nirvana*, 221)

he admits at times
to feeling
like a fraud;
maybe he doesn't
deserve this turn of fortune.
sometimes he feels
guilty about it all.
in much of his
later work, he wrote
about his new home & life
& how uneventful
it was
or he wrote about the
past, always
the past.
he writes about
what he used to
do, how he used to

be, how things
were crazy & full
of life,
how the struggle was
much better,
there was no
edge, & now
the edge is gone
w/ his comfort.
in "barstool," he decides

   the longer I live the more I realize
   that I knew exactly what I was doing
    (*Betting on the Muse*, 283)

but it often seems,
it this latter work,
he misses the struggling,
drunk, uncertain years.
he handles it with grace
& humor, though, as
seen in the poem
"why oh why oh why not?"
in *Slouching toward nirvana*…

   it happened slow and it happened fast: from   idiot to
   successful idiot.
    (227)

some of his most humorous
writing was when
he switched from a typewriter

to a Macintosh computer.

   I just moved the poems
   over
   and dropped them into
   the trash can

he writes in "the trash can"
adding with snide wisdom,

   It's always better
   to reject yourself before
   the editors do.
    (*Muse*, 327)

the switchover wasn't
a smooth one, however.
in "it got away," he complains

   Lost another poem
   in this computer.
   it's like reeling in
   a fish
   and then it
   escapes the hook
    (*Muse*, 375)

not knowing how to
use a computer,
he takes classes
to figure it out,
noting the irony of it
all, of course,
here he is, an old

man & famous
writer, taking a class
with housewives & kids,
wondering what he's
doing with technology,[13]
when in the past he was
just fine with pencil and paper
and rusty old manual "typers"
as he often
called them.

> yet twice
> I found myself
> with a typewriter.
> I wrote a short
> story which was
> accepted by
> a leading
> magazine

he writes in
"confessions of a
genius"
(*Betting on the Muse*, p. 310)

---

[13] In his *The Captain is Out to Lunch and the Sailors Have Taken Over the Ship*, his journal entries, he writes on October 9, 1991: "Computer class was a kick for sore balls. You pick it up inch by inch and try to get the totality. The problem is that the books say one way and some people say the other. The terminology slowly becomes understandable. The computer only does, it doesn't know. You can confuse it and it can turn on you. It's up to you to get along with it. Still, the computer can go crazy and do odd and strange things. It can catch viruses, get shorts, bombs out, etc" (p. 45).

but then confesses he hocked the typer for money and
stopped writing.

& yet
talking about those
hard & lost times,
the tone is nostalgic,
he misses those
times,
when life felt
more real, when there
was no comfort,
when he never dreamt
that one day he
would be an international
famous writer
driving a BMW
owning his own
house,
the old man who

pays over $20,000 in quarterly tax and still
manage
to write some of the best poetry
of our time.

(*Slouching*, p. 227)

No one could accuse
him of not being
self-actualized in his
autumnal years.

4. CHOOSE YOUR OWN BUKOWSKI

like Picasso, there are many
Bukowskis to choose from,
different eras.
do you prefer the cube or blue period?
there is the early poet Bukowski,
Crucifix in a Deathhand era,
the early & mid 1960s,
when he wrote more lyrical, imagistic
poetry & published with all
the obscure small magazines,
chapbooks coming
from Loujon Press,
those limited
editions worth
tens of thousands
of dollars from
collectors today.

there is the late 60s-early 70s
L.A. Free Press &
Notes of a Dirty Old Man
Bukowski, an underground
cult name in the city
but still not widely known.
some of his greatest experimental writing
came out of that period
as well as his
first novel,
Post Office.

then there is the

THE DIRTY REALISM DUO

Carlton Way Bukowski,
writing his second
& third novels
& the best of his
poetry. he was at his
prime,
getting ready for
going big time
in
his career, in his
mid-50s &
having paid his dues.

there is the early 1980s
Ham of Rye period,
the novel reflective,
more traditional,
about events of his childhood,
the sort of coming-of-age
autobiography that
all writers must publish,
either early or late
in their careers,
but never
in the middle.

we then have the late 1980s
post-*Barfly* Bukowski,
the movie a minor hit,
an instant indie cult
classic,
Mickey Rourke playing a

far better Bukowski than
Matt Dillon in
Factotum.

there is
the 1990s Bukowski,
with the novel *Hollywood,*
the poems about the past
& computers
& wishing for a different
time, a more lively time,
but not regretting what
he has now.

finally,
there is the posthumous Bukowski,
with the novel *Pulp,*
which should have never
been published,
& the hundreds of poems
left behind,
generating books
for more than a decade so that
the publishers (Ecco/HarperCollins
having bought out the list) can
continue to make a lot
of money off substandard poetry,
work Bukowski intentionally stated
could only be published
after his death.

a dead man does not care

about poor
work being in print,
as long as it brings an
income to the dear wife
who survived him.

i prefer the
Carton Way Bukowski,
which is probably obvious,
the Bukowski making
that transition from
one mode of life to another,
yet still maintaining
a sense of integrity,
as he claims in "good news,"

> You will not find me at
> literary gatherings
> holding a cocktail
> glass.
>   (*Slouching*, 232-233)

it's fun to imagine Buk
@ a *Paris Review* party
@ Elaine's
or on *The Tonight
Show.*

what would he say—

better yet, what poems
would he have
written about

George Plimpton
& Johnny Carson, Jay Leno,

or David Letterman
just as he wrote about

Faye Dunaway's legs?

8.

POST-KAFKA:
ON BUKOWSKI'S COCKROACHES

"Never take your eyes off the roach," Bukowski admonishes in the poem "there once was a woman who put her head into an oven" from *Love Is a Dog from Hell* (line 11, p. 131), musing on the strength and superior survival ability of the insect. Bukowski has written many poems about roaches, as much as he has written about being drunk, women, betting on horses, and failed, violent, sad relationships. After a life of rooming houses and run-down apartments in East Hollywood (before money and fame came his way), it is likely he spent a significant amount of time living with roaches. He claims in "in the neighborhood of murder": "the roaches spit out/paperclips" (*Love Is a Dog from Hell*, lines 1-2, p. 227). One of Bukowski's common motifs in his poetry is describing his surroundings as he sits down, beer or wine bottles on the table by the "typer" as he was fond of calling typewriters, Brahms or Beethoven on the radio or record player—and plenty of roaches scuttling by on the floor or wall. So it was inevitable that he would write about them, even come to admire them. Sometimes, however, as he notes in "thoughts on an evening when gray walls breathe and huff," there

> hasn't been a roach in here in
> week
> or a woman, either (lines 15-17)[14]

In "cockroach," also from *Love Is in a Dog from Hell,* be considers the theory that one day the roach "tribe is going to/inherit the earth" (lines 26-27, p. 105) as he struggles to kill one of the bugs as

> I then got a can and sprayed
> and sprayed and sprayed
> and finally the roach came out
> and gave me a very dirty look. (lines 7-10)

The "dirty look" does not stop Bukowski from killing his unwanted roommate "because I paid the rent/and he didn't" (lines 15-16). Bukowski is reaffirming that man is the master of the world, not the roach, no matter what their numbers. He expounds on this in another poem, "death of the roach," where he kills a rival for real estate again:

> the roach climbs
> (the mirrors of love are broken)
> blind yet begotten with life, a dedicated wraith

---

[14] According to www.bukowski.net, this poem has not been included in any collections yet, nor has been published in a zine or journal.

of pus and antennae. (lines 20-23)[15]

He has also written poems about spiders and flies, insects that also invade his space; these poems comprise an ethnography—to coin an anthropological term—of the relationship between humans and bugs. There is no avoiding it: both must share the world, despite the fact there is no symbiosis or harmony. Most humans will kill the bugs that come into their domestic dwellings; those who do not believe in taking a life will just scoot them out the door or window, back to the outside world.

Bukowski affords the roach human traits; one gives him "a very dirty look" and another is "begotten with life." This is in his imagination, since roaches do not create facial expresses and most likely are not aware of existentialism; Bukowski is simply projecting what he would feel if some giant bug tried spraying him with poison or crushing him. After all, the roach is simply existing and surviving the way it was designed—what did it ever do to deserve to be gassed, flattened, and killed like a criminal? The reader identifies with Bukowski, however, and not the roach, as humans conditionally find roaches to be dirty and disgusting, as stated in "the death of roach" when Bukowski tosses the dead bug into the toilet and "flush[es] his ugliness away" (line 29, p. 119). This, I contend, was the initial popularity of Kafka's *The Metamorphosis*—not for themes of the loss of identity, imprisonment, and loneliness, but for the simple reason that readers recognized the

---

[15] Although published posthumously, this poem was originally published in 1959 in the small press zine *EPOS* (vol. 11, no. 2) and his 1965 chapbook, *Cold Dogs in the Courtyard*. The lyrical, imagistic style is considerably different from his prosaic style Bukowski is best known for.

dislike of insects. Helmuth Kaiser, in his essay "Kafka's Fantasy of Punishment," notes that Gregor Samsa has become "a loathsome disgusting creature" and

> It is no accident that the animal in this case is an insect [...] As far as the development of disgust is concerned, there exists at first an anal pleasure, which is entirely free of disgust. With the repression of anal pleasure, a disgust for feces arises. As long as the pressure is not yet consolidated, the disgust is violent (151).

Roaches are often found in bathrooms, near toilets, as seen in "cockroach." Bukowski is urinating and when he spots the roach "he hauled his butt/into a crack." By alluding to anal images, Bukowski's abhorrence does become violent. If he did not equate the roach with filth and feces, as Kaiser points out, he would probably not care that the cockroach was there, and would have let it go in peace. Bukowski claims in "the death of a roach": "the insects are suspect—/man can only destroy himself" (lines 44-45, p. 119). By killing insects, people try to remove the instilled and learned repressions ("the mirrors of love are broken") so they can feel pure and without repugnance. The cockroach, then, as exhibited by both Kafka and Bukowski, becomes a scapegoat for the emancipation from refuse and a means to returning to an infant, innocent state of anal pleasure.

9.

"SOME PICNIC"

One of Bukowski's best-known, trademark poems is "some picnic" from *Play the Piano Drunk/Like a Percussion instrument/Until the Fingers Begin to Bleed a Bit* (1979), originally published in *The Wormwood Review* 14. 3, 55 (1974), a small literary journal composed on an electric typewriter that, each issue, would publish entire sections (chapbooks) of poetry by Bukowski, Lyn Lifshin, Gerald Locklin, Steve Richmond, and other little magazine luminaries of the time. The poem is another fine example of Dirty Realism. He writes about Jane, whom he was living with for seven years,

> she was drunk
> I loved her (lines 3-4, p.24)

At a picnic, his parents are ice to he, even though she is drinking. They have a nice time, "everybody laughed/I didn't laugh" (lines 16-17, p. 24). Later, he cannot figure out why their attitude toward her changed. Jane calls him a "damn fool" for not figuring it out—for a writer, he wasn't paying much attention. She says, "they kept looking at my

THE DIRTY REALISM DUO

beer-belly/they think I'm pregnant" (lines 27-28, pp. 24-25). In true Dirty Realist fashion, Bukowski toasts to their "beautiful child." While amusing, there is an undertone of sadness here—if his parents really do believe Jane is pregnant, they might be happy that they will become grandparents, and what will they think when they find out otherwise?

10.

CARVER ON BUKOWSKI

Carver's "You Don't Know What Love Is" is an homage to his fellow Dirty Realist, written after Carver went to a reading of Bukowski's at the University of Santa Cruz. It is a monologue, intended to be Bukowski speaking to the audience while he is reading poetry. Or is the poem he's reading? It could be both; he's talking about having a lover half his age.

> I got this young broad see she's beautiful
> She calls me Bukowski
> Bukowski she says in this little voice (lines 25-38)[16]

He adores this young lady, but she also seems to annoy him, asking why he likes to listen to classical music, why he likes to drink so much, why he likes to spend hours and

---

[16] The poem is included in *All of Us,* but I am quoting from a photocopy of the original manuscript in my possession, so no page numbers are given.

hours behind his typewriter. He knows she will never understand. The writer's life is a lonely but good one, explains:

> and I look out the window onto DeLongpre Avenue
> and I see people walking up and down the sidewalk
> (lines 71-80)

Carver must have been paying good attention to recall what street Bukowski lived on, and this dates the poem. Bukowski lived at 5126½ DeLongpre, in Los Angeles (the edge of East Hollywood, zip code 92007), for a short while in 1965, with his pregnant wife, Frances Smith. He then moved to 5124 DeLongpre Avenue from 1965 to 1973, according to the timeline listed at www.bukowski. net. In "the strangest sight you ever did see—" from *Love Is a Dog from Hell*,[17] Bukowski writes:

> I had this room in front on DeLongpre and I
> used to sit for hours... (p. 225)

Carver has the voice of Bukowski going on about how "I'm 51 years old and she's 25/and we're in love and she's jealous" (lines 86-87), how lucky he feels, how good it is to be in love, or at least to have a woman that young to make love to.

It is possible that Bukowski's "my groupie" (also in *Love Is a Dog from Hell*) is from the same reading "out-

---

[17] For Bukowski scholars, the poem originally appeared in small press zine *Poetry Now #6* (1974). Bukowski was no longer living at DeLongpre but Carlton Way in 1974.

side of Santa Cruz" (line 2). He is almost done with the reading when a

Young girl came running toward me
Long gown & divine eyes of fire
And she leaped up on the stage
And screamed: "I WANT YOU!
I WANT YOU! TAKE ME!" (lines 16-20)

I like to think that if Carver was there, he was watching closely and taking notes.

THE DIRTY REALISM DUO

PART III

RAY

like a rocket shot into the
night sky
    ---Charles Bukowski, "bedpans"

11.

ABOUT DIRTY REALISM: A MEDITATION ON RAYMOND CARVER'S "GAZEBO"

METHOD

The inspiration comes from several sources— Vladimir Nabokov's *Pale Fire*, of course, and Samuel R. Delany's *The American Shore* (Delany refers to *Pale Fire* as a predecessor of the form, as well as Roland Bathes' *S/Z*). These are reflexive, meditative texts where the life of the writer mingles with the work under critical scrutiny—fictional with Nabokov and real with Delany, devoting more than 300 pages to a single Thomas Disch story, "Angouleme," from *334*. I know in my heart I could do the same for the Raymond Carver story that is the subject study, "Gazebo," and in fact I considered following Delany's path and writing an entire book; instead, I present nearly 10,000 words on a 2,500 words short story. I have employed the theory, and practice, of critifiction, as coined by Raymond Federman, "discourse…that is critical as well as fictional" (*Critifictions: Postmodern Essays* 49).

There is little that is fiction in this essay, however, other than Carver's story (which is autobiographical) and the inquiry into the validity of my memories, something that Federman takes into consideration regarding all writing that has to do with the writer's personal past: how true can our biased autobiographies be? "I am in the process of burying Postmodernism," Federman explains (107), calling for the funeral of dead forms of critical theory because "discourse impregnate us," admonishing the "importance of always questioning, always doubting, always challenging these discourses" (48), as well as memory. I have also been influenced by two critifictional texts: Frank Lentricchia's *Lecchesi and the Whale* and Avital Ronell's *Crack Wars*. Both works engage the genre to study a single literary classic: *Moby-Dick* for Lentricchia and *Madame Bovary* for Ronell. Lentricchia, while being one of the world's leading Don DeLillo scholars, was also a champion of *close reading*, rejecting the New Criticism in his *After the New Criticism*, a landmark and controversial work in its own right (at the time of publication). Just as Federman was turning his back on modernist structuralism, Lentricchia was also calling for alternative forms of dissertation to match the evolution of literature in the later part of the twentieth century. Not using the exact terminology, he too was employing critifiction in *Lecchesi and the Whale*, where a college professor has a mid-life breakdown while "teaching" Melville's leviathan text, relating the unfortunate matters of Melville's life (*Moby-Dick* was initially a financial and critical flop, after several seafaring adventure yarns that brought the writer money and nominal fame) to his own situation: the financial and critical failure of his experimental fiction. (After complaints from students that "each of his fifty-minute class hours started with an exceedingly slow call of the roll, a kind of chant, followed by a twenty-two minute silence" (37), the administration suggests he takes the semester off and not endanger his tenure.) Ronell advises the reader "this work does not accord with literary criticism in the traditional sense" (49). Riddled with semiotic maxims and quotes from Heidegger and Nietzsche, the center of *Crack Wars* reveals an essay on drug addiction and *Madam Bovary* that is "found" in the future, inside a time capsule buried in ice; written by a long gone, forgotten, dead academic known as Avital Ronell—essentially, however, the text is "a work on Madam Bovary, and nothing more" (49). In the same spirit, this critical essay is a work on "Gazebo" and nothing more other than why I find it personally effective and affecting—I identify with the text, yes; I see parallels of my life in the lives of the fictional characters, which are autobiographical objects from Carver's personal history. Is this not the criteria for the best fiction—when the reader is left facing the Borgesian mirror? Finally, this essay follows in the footsteps of Jane Tompkins' groundbreaking "Me and My Shadow," an ambivalent essay about the rigid rules of academic discourse and a love-hate relationship with the scholarly, the memoir, and the creative. The literary critic, Thompkins contends, is

> the same person who feels and who discourses about epistemology. The problem is that you can't talk about your private life in the course of doing your professional work. You have to pretend that epistemology, or whatever you're writing about, has nothing to do with your life, that

it's more exalted, more important, because it supposedly transcends the merely personal. Well, I'm tired of the conventions that keep discussions of epistemology, or James Joyce, segregated from meditations on what is happening outside my window or inside my heart. The public-private dichotomy, which is to say, the public-private hierarchy, is a founding condition of female oppression. I say to hell with it. The reason I feel embarrassed at my own attempts to speak personally in a professional context is that I have been conditioned to feel that way (25).

And so I approach Raymond Carver's "Gazebo" in similar manner, comparing events, feelings, and dialogues from my past to situations, emotions, and spoken words in the story, because, like Thompkins, the abstractions and issues in "Gazebo" "are already personal for me without being personalized [by Carver] [...] they concern things I've been thinking about for some time, struggling with, trying to figure out for myself" (36). I begin with commentary on individual sentences, much like John Shade reflexively examines Charles Kinbote's "Pale Fire" line-by-line.

A DIRTY DOZEN

1.That morning, she pours Teacher's over my belly and licks it off.
The opening sentence, a curious action, sets up the possibility of an erotic story. Carver doesn't go into further detail, however, like a work of porn fiction would; he doesn't talk about how she (her name is Holly, but we won't

know this until the sentence) licks it off. Did some get into his belly button and she sucked it out like one would do a body shot on Spring Break or during Mardi Gras? What sounds did she make? The fact that she is licking up straight bourbon off the narrator's flesh is an indication that she's a pretty heavy alcoholic, and she likes her booze. When I first read this story, and that sentence, sometime in, oh, 1987 I believe it was, I thought: I'd like to try that sometime. It brought to mind my ex-girlfriend Gretchen, who, when I came too much as she gave me a blowjob, and some of my semen would fly out of her mouth and onto my stomach and into my belly button, she would lick it off my skin. She would giggle and play with it, get it between her fingers, a sticky mess like the web of a spider. The fourteen-year-old Janet Rose, in Gordon Lish's *Dear Mr. Capote*, did something similar, taking the narrator's semen in her mouth and exchanging in back and forth during a kiss (and Lish was Carver's editor, who edited "Gazebo" so heavily, that it reads like Lish's prose). Oh yes, this sentence made me both nostalgic and libidinous and wanting for another time, my teenage years, when, being young and full of protein, I would have massive, thick ejaculations every time I had sex, especially with Gretchen, my first true love, a fragile, bird-like blonde girl who always had big dreams for our future, a future that never happened, a future that I mourned, a future that only existed in a parallel universe. I had introduced the works of Raymond Carver to my buddy Jordan Faris, whom I once was in a band with—he was the lead singer and I was the guitar player and for two years we (and a bass player and drummer, always new members) played gigs up and down California, and like Gretchen, we had big dreams, and like Gretchen, we mapped out a future where we would be rock stars and get on the cover of Rolling Stone (as the song goes). That never happened, and by the time I gave Jordan a copy of *What We Talk About When We Talk About Love*, there was no more band—I had returned to college for a short while and he was married to a crazy woman who always had tabs of LSD to give us when we wanted it. On reading the story, he said, "What's Teacher's?" I said, "Some kind of booze." He asked if I ever tried it and I said no; I had, in fact, looked for it in liquor stores but none of them ever seemed to carry it. One time we were at a hotel bar and asked the bartender if he had it and he said yes. We tried it and we liked it. Jordan and I used to make up drinks so we made one up that night: Coke, a splash of cranberry juice, and two shots of Teacher's (one for Holly, one for Duane): we called it a Raymond Carver.

2. That afternoon she tries to jump out the window.

Holly is obviously suicidal. Whether she is serious about jumping out the window and causing harm to her or just being melodramatic is uncertain. She *does* seem *try* to do it. Is she simply trying to "get" to him? In this sentence, Carver forces us to look into our own past for experiences that can we can relate to and reflect on. Someone who has never experienced being suicidal or being with someone who is suicidal probably will not understand the ugliness of it all. I believe Maryanne Burk Carver tells the experience that inspired this story in her memoir, *What it Used to Be Like*, recounting her twenty-five years of marriage to Raymond Carver. In Chapter 13, "That August," Carver goes off to Montana without her, and when he returns, he confesses he slept with another woman. To discuss the matter of his infidelity away from their children, Mrs. Carver writes:

> Ray and I went off to the local Howard Johnson's motel. He fortified himself at the shabby little liquor store a block from the house, buying half a gallon of vodka, bottles or orange and grapefruit juice.... In the motel room we drank as we talked, until we could sleep. When Ray was finally out, I got up and went into the bathroom and locked the door. I felt as if someone had kicked me in the stomach" (256).

The opening of "Gazebo" has a man and a woman dealing with his infidelity (he screwed the motel maid) by drinking, talking, and having sex. They're a young couple and they run a motel. Carver and his wife never operated a motel, but he did hold down many menial blue-collar jobs, from janitor to sawmill worker. When I first read that sentence, it reminded me of Jennifer, my girlfriend senior year of high school; we had gotten into a big fight and she thought I had broken up with her so she took the pills in her friend's medicine bottle. I forget what the pills were, there were about six or eight. She showed up at my door and said she was going to die. She was crying. I was glad my parents weren't there. My best friend, Maurice, was. He had a car and I didn't. We drove her to her friend's house, the friend whose pills she had taken.[18] I called a

---

[18] It is here the story gets complicated. Jennifer was an adopted child and her mother often hit her. She left her mother's house and was emancipated at seventeen (she could write her own notes to excuse herself

suicide hotline and told them what the medication was. They said she'd be all right, that we should walk her around and give her coffee but she was going to be okay and maybe she should see a counselor at school. That was the past. The present, now, as I write this study, I am reminded of the woman I just got out of a relationship with. Liv, *Liv Kellgren*. She is bipolar, has been diagnosed bipolar when she was fifteen, after she tried to commit suicide when she had an abortion. I learned, this past summer, when we were estranged from each other, that she tried to kill herself again, at age thirty-three. This information was passed along to me. I had to know if it were true. I was not surprised to hear the news. I sent her emails, I left messages, I asked how she was, I hinted that I knew something was wrong, I didn't want to outright ask: "Did you try to take your life last summer?" She did not respond to my queries. I pressed the issue, I had to know, I told her I was worried, I told her I could help. She sent an email: *You'd like it if I were dead, wouldn't you? You would laugh.* I told her no, no, I would not; I said my soul would be destroyed if she ever did that.

3. I go, Holly, this can't continue.
Carver establishes the quirky present-tense style he uses to narrate this fiction. Instead of "says" or "asks" the verbs are "go" and "goes." I am reminded of John Clellon Holmes' beat novel *Go*, although there is nothing about "Gazebo" that has anything to do with the Beats. It's just the title. Most likely the use of the verb *go* was via the edi-

---

from school). Her friend's parents said she could live with them until she graduated. It was not an ideal situation. I was so in love with her I put up with it, not realizing how horrible this all was.

torial hand of Gordon Lish, as I mentioned when discussing the first sentence. (Martha Giles recollects taking a fiction workshop with Carver in 1980: "He told us how he had sat in on a trial in California where a girl on the witness stand kept saying, 'and then he goes,' 'and then I go.' He coveted these cozy usages, and this particular one shows up in 'Gazebo'.") There is significant documentation and debate as to the extent that Gordon Lish, Carver's friend and editor at *Esquire* and Knopf, edited and re-titled Carver's work, and if the editorial hand was reaching into the gray zone of actual co-authorship. In D. T. Max's article, "The Carver Chronicles," he notes that Lish had been publicly confessing to what in essence may have been ghostwriting, but he was not being taken seriously and:

> Seven years ago, Lish arranged for the sale of his papers to the Lilly Library at Indiana University. Since then, only a few Carver scholars have examined the Lish manuscripts thoroughly. When one tried to publish his conclusions, Carver's widow and literary executor, the poet Tess Gallagher, effectively blocked him with copyright cautions and pressure.

Max examined the archive papers himself and found evidence, on edited Carver manuscripts, that this assertion looked to be true. Max interviewed Lish in New York:

> We sat across from each other at his kitchen table and I asked him what had happened. "I don't like talking about the Carver period," he said, "because of my sustained sense of his betrayal and because it seems bad form to discuss

this [...] [and] puts me in an absolutely impossible light," he continued. "I can only be despised for my participation."

G.P. Lainsbury points out in *The Carver Chronotope*: "It is now the established opinion that that Lish's editorial tampering with Carver's work constitutes and integral part of Carver's writerly narrative of recovery and self-assertion rather than some sort of critical indictment" (146). Lish befriended Raymond Carver in the early 1960s while he was director of linguistic studies at Behavioral Research Laboratories in Menlo Park, California. Carver, who had published a handful of poems and short stories in small literary journals, was unknown, hopeful, and unsuspecting that Lish would help him become one of the greatest American writers of the twentieth century, the acknowledged father of the minimalist movement, although that was a label he never cared for and even moved away from.[19] A hard drinking blue collar worker, married early,

---

[19] In *Minimalism and the Short Story: Raymond Carver, Amy Hempel, and Mary Robinson*, Cynthia J. Whitney Hallet argues: "Minimalist short fiction is part of that design of the short story as defined by Poe, characterized by Chekhov, and refined by Hemingway which eventually emerged fully formed in the fiction of Carver" (15). For some critics, minimalism is a four letter word, and for some writers, a scarlet letter. Carver did not care being pigeon-holed as such. Michael Trussler, in "The Narrowed Voice: Raymond Carver and Minimalism," attests that critics are "so captivated...with the term's (supposed) ability to provide precise and final demarcation, that it seems paradoxical to discover the myriad of widely diverse cultural activities jointly labeled by the 'minimalist' aesthetic....the term is used pejoratively, a rapid dismissal of an artwork, often made more on moral than stylistic grounds" (23). "A critical appreciation of the term," counters Hallet, "minimalism is not a negative literary evaluation...[but] an elaborate

with two children, and never enough money to pay the rent and bills, he was just trying to get by, holding onto a dream that his writing would someday be noticed. When Lish became the fiction editor of *Esquire* in 1969, he made sure a larger, literate audience sat up and took notice of Raymond Carver. Lish did not edit Carver's *Cathedral* the way he did with the two previous collections. According to D. T. Max,

> [Carver] insisted that if Lish wanted to edit his next collection, he would have to keep his hands off. "I can't undergo [that] kind of surgical amputation and transplantation," he wrote Lish in August 1982. "Please help me with this book as a good editor, the best ... not as my ghost," he pleaded two months later. Lish reluctantly complied. "So be it," he wrote in December 1982 after giving the manuscript to *Cathedral* only a light edit.

4. "This has got to stop."

The narrator, Duane, having cheated on Holly, has no business asking her to calm down. He's the one who transgressed; she's the one who is hurt and frantic. It reminds me of the married woman I was having an affair with, her name was Christine, when I was living with an-

---

arrangement of vernacular and trope that appears as concrete details which reflect complex states of being and which correlate with elements of the universal human condition" (47). Steven J. McDermott, on his website *StoryGlossia*, disputes: "'Popular Mechanics' is a metafictional rejoinder to the critics who've labeled him a minimalist, which reflects a major concern of Carver's when he published *Where I'm Calling from*: He wanted to present his work in a broader perspective, illustrate that the *minimalism*—a label which he rejected—was just a technique used in some stories, not the defining characteristic of his work."

other woman, her name was Karin. Karin eventually kicked me out of the apartment, not because of the affair (which she had no idea about but I suspect she suspected) bit for the plain reason that I was a bum and wasn't paying my part of our living expenses. Misusing her credit card was another matter. It is my intention to be completely honest in this critifiction, as Carver is honest in his own fiction. I was a bad boyfriend. I was drinking a lot and doing crystal meth. Christine left her husband so she could be with me. She liked to drink and do drugs with me and we'd have sex and get crazy the way Duane and Holly get crazy in the motel room. One time I said to Christine, "Pour some wine into my navel and suck it out," and she did. She asked what made me think of that and I told her about the Carver story "Gazebo." "I'd like to read that story someday," she said. Anyway, after Karin had kicked me out and I was living with Christine, I had to go over to Karin's to get some of my stuff and I told Christine I had no idea when I would be back. Christine thought I was going to sleep with Karin and she jumped up and started hitting me in the face with her fists, crying, calling me names. This wasn't the first time this happened. I pushed her away, my face numb, and said, "This has got to stop."

5. We are sitting on the sofa in one of the upstairs suites.
Regarding the incident described in the previous sentence, I was sitting on the sofa when Christine hit me. But let's move away from that scene of sudden domestic violence. I would like to discuss the nature and history of "the sofa."

6. There were any number of vacancies to choose from.

120

Christine didn't like to have sex on the bed I shared with Karin. "I can smell her on the sheets and pillow," she said; "I know you both made love there last night; I can't make love with you on the same bed." There was also the chance that Karin might come home, unexpected, unannounced, because she'd done this before. I couldn't go over to Christine's because she lived with her husband and that was too dangerous, and for her: too weird. So we did what married people have done time immortal: we went to motel rooms. Sometimes we'd do it in her car but motel rooms were better, especially the Dolphin Motel that had mirrors on the ceiling and five channels of porno to watch. There were always vacancies in the middle of the day; people having affairs only came by at night (unlike us) and the other occupants were call girls waiting for the next john. Christine said she felt like a hooker going there and that turned her on.

7. But we needed a suite, a place to move around in and be able to talk.
Christine and I got a suite on her birthday. It had a Jacuzzi in it. She didn't want to have sex. "I just want you to hold me and tell me I'm beautiful," she said. "Kiss me all over and hold me, please, and pretend that this is love."

8. So we locked up the motel office that morning and gone upstairs to a suite.
There was one time, before Christine left her husband, that we went to a three-hour motel near the center of the city.

9. She goes, "Duane, this is killing me."

"I want to get out of this relationship alive," Karin said one night, crying, curled up in the bed, "this relationship is going to kill me and I won't let that happen." People wanting out are a common theme in Carver's fiction—out of a marriage, out of situation, out of the choices they've made. In Holly's case, she wants out so much that she intends to kill herself, to end the pain in her heart. When Karin said that to me, it was like a slap in the face—did she really mean that, did she really think that about me, and was I some kind of terrible person, some asshole, that she had to run away from, fearful of her survival? It did not make me feel good. I imagine that Duane does not feel good about himself, either, considering Holly's draconian behavior and reaction to the betrayal. What can a man do in a situation such as this other than to pour another drink and accept the fact that he is a jerk.

10. We are drinking Teacher's with ice and water.
Ah, Teacher's again, a curious alcohol. I have a hard time finding it these days, either in liquor stores or bars. With all that drinking going on, I imagine Duane and Holly were quite sloshed, sauced, and three sheets to wind. Then again, perhaps not. They are heavy drinkers, Duane notes this later in the story:

> Drinking's funny. When I look back on it, all of our important decisions have been figured out when we were drinking. Even when we talked about having to cut back on our drinking, we'd be sitting at the kitchen table or at our picnic table with a six-pack our whiskey (107).

11. We'd slept a while between morning and afternoon.

I seldom wake up before noon—this is the writer's way, my way, up all night, sometimes four or five a.m., writing the next novel, the next personal essay, the next play, the next poem or critical text.[20] Sometimes I go through phases where I get to bed around midnight and wake up at seven or eight a.m., and my days are different, longer—not as productive, but more aware, as if I have come out of al alcoholic haze with a only a mild hangover.

12. Then she was out of the bed and threatening to climb out the window in her undergarments.

This indeed, again, shows how suicidal Holly is, and how hurt she is by what Duane has done. It is an image can break your heart—a woman *with* a broken heart falling out a window in her bra and panties like the falling man in Don DeLillo's *Falling Man*. It reminds me of the night Christine told me our relationship was dead, over; she was standing at the top of the stairs in her condo, I was lying on the couch with her cats and watching TV. She was wearing a nightshirt that barely went past her hips. She was not wearing panties and from the top of the stairs, I had a direct view of her shaved vagina. "There's nothing left anymore," she said, "there's nothing in my heart for you," she said, and all I could do is stare at her genitalia and wonder why it looked like a stranger's sex, not my lover's. I felt dirty looking at her.

---

[20] It is 4:10 A.M., on February 19, 2008, as I write this sentence. The Cartoon Network's *Adult Swim* is on the TV and Coast to Coast AM is on the radio. The rent is late, as always, and my cats are staring at me.

REFLECTIONS ON DIRTY REALISM

I have to stop here. While it would be interesting to comment on every sentence in "Gazebo," like John Shade, I would have an entire book instead of an essay, as I stated at the beginning; however, there would be issues of copyright and permissions if I went that far. Would Carver's window, Tess Gallagher, allow me to quote, essentially reprint, the entire story, and how much the agency that handles literary rights for the Carver estate, charge me, even for a word of scholarship? Journals and academic presses do not pay for the permission fees, the writer does, so if said writer/scholar does not have the personal funds to pay for reprint rights, said writer/scholar must pay attention to the amount of quoted words used. Fair use doctrine allows for no more than 500 quoted words. There are 124 words in those first twelve sentences, so if I am going to quote any further, which I will, I need to stop there.

From my own life, as I vetted these twelve sentences, I seem to have called up two relationships that I had at the same time—living with one woman while having an affair with a married woman, just as Duane has two women in his life: a wife and a maid. Duane has lost them both; the maid has stopped coming to work, he doesn't know where she is, and Holly does not appear ready to forgive him, wanting to escape to Nevada. Similarly, I lost both women—my girlfriend found out about the married woman, and the married woman lost interest in me after I was truly available, rather than the guilty pleasure of illicit encounters.

Next to "Popular Mechanics," "Gazebo" is the most difficult Carver story for me to read. I have been in these situations, I have had fights like this, and I already stated, I strongly identify with Duane and Holly's relationship, or the end of it. When I see my history in these words, I do not remember the best parts of my life. What I remember is ugly, ungainly, and dirty. This is why "Gazebo" is the essence of Dirty Realism as practiced by Carver: blue-collar American lives so filled with ennui that it takes an incident of the seemingly grotesque, a social oddity, for a person to reach epiphany. "My life is going to change," the narrator of "Fat" states in the last sentence, because he *needs* to alter the monotony that has imprisoned his being, just as Holly needs to escape the prison that is failed marriage—the suite she and Duane are in is a prison, and her attempt to leap out the window, braving injury or death, was a symbolic act of the prison break. Duane, stopping her, plays the role of prison guard, perhaps warden; he is not going to let her go, not this early, not this soon, not until there is some kind of closure—of course, his agenda is talk her out of leaving him, to make amends for his transgression. If she leaves him, what will he have? Nothing, and he is afraid of that.

THE END OF SOME THINGS

In Arthur F. Bethea's "Raymond Carver's Inheritance from Ernest Hemingway's Literary Technique," the critic compares and contrasts many Carver stories with Hemingway's work, showing where there is influence in passages, theme, and approach. Bethea disappoints, however, by failing to point out a very obvious, very telling sentence in "Gazebo." "We'd reached the end of something" (108). This sentence refers to the Nick Adams story, "The End of

Something" from *In Our Time*. This is another Carver nod to Hemingway. Carver tells Larry McCaffery and Sinda Gregory in an interview:

> I didn't read him until I was in college and then I read the wrong book (*Across the River and into the Trees*) and didn't like him very much. But a little later I read *In Our Time* in a class and I found that he was marvelous. I remember thinking, This is *it*; if you can write prose like this, you've done something (75).

Both "Gazebo" and "The End of Something" are essentially the same length, less than 2,500 words, and share a common theme: the demise of a relationship; one is a marriage and the other is a young romance. "The End of Something" handles the situation with dignity while "Gazebo" is handled with shame. "The End of Something" is calm and subtle as opposed to the nervous energy of Carver's story. Nick and Marjorie take a rowboat out to fish for trout. It is something they have apparently done many times before. Hemingway's doesn't explain who Marjorie is—obviously a girlfriend, but not how long they've been together, where and how they met or what their plans are. The same can be said for Carver's Duane and Holly—these are simply people dealing with the end of their relationships. Nick has chosen this moment to break up with Marjorie; he's brooding about how best to do it. She has no idea what's coming. She asks him twice: "What's the matter?" and both times he says: "I don't know" (38, 40). She *might* know what's coming, however; Nick keeps telling her, "You know everything" and she continues to press him to tell her why he is acting strangely: "Go on and say it" (40). When he finally does tell her, she doesn't act surprised; she accepts it.

Holly does not accept Duane's infidelity. The more she thinks about it, the more it destroys her soul: "'Something's died in me,' she goes. 'It took a long time for it to do it, but it's dead. You've killed something, just like you'd taken an axe to it'" (106). Nick's admission is similar: "'I feel as though everything was gone to hell inside of me. I don't know, Marge. I don't know what to say'" (40).

Both Carver and Hemingway are autobiographical writers and these stories were influenced by some event or situation in their respective lives. Critic Kenneth Lynn suggests "The End of Something" is about Hemingway and his first wife, Hadley, and that Nick's statement "it isn't fun anymore" is how Hemingway felt about his marriage. Maryanne Burk Carver recounts her twenty-five years of marriage to Carver and pinpoints and event similar to the situation in "Gazebo." In Chapter 13 of her memoir, *What It Was Like*, Carver goes off to Montana without her, and when he returns, he tells her he slept with another woman. To discuss the matter of his infidelity away from their children, Mrs. Carver writes:

> Ray and I went off to the local Howard Johnson's motel. He fortified himself at the shabby little liquor store a block from the house, buying half a gallon of vodka, bottles or orange and grapefruit juice....In the motel room we drank as we talked, until we could sleep. When Ray was finally out, I got up and went into the bathroom and locked the door. I felt as if someone had kicked me in the stomach" (256).

She doesn't say that this part of their marriage became "Gazebo" but the similarities are too obvious.

Marjorie takes the boat and leaves Nick. She has accepted the fact that this is the end. When Nick says he will push the boat off for her, she replies: "You don't need to" (41). Holly, at the end of "Gazebo" and calmed down, has accepted the end of her marriage by remembering an encounter she and Duane had while driving through Yakima, Washington. They had stopped off at a house and asked for a drink of water, where a kind elderly couple welcomed them and fed them cake. Holly says: "'I thought we'd be like that too when we got old enough. Dignified. And people would come to out door'" (109). Marjorie also reminiscences as she and Nick are in the boat; she points out their "old ruin" and asks him: "Can you remember when it was a mill?" (36) just as Holly inquires: "You remember the time we drove to that old farm place…out past Terrace Heights?" (109) That seems to be the way things tend to come to an end, when people recall better times, past moments that ear-mark when there was love, rather than emptiness.

"Dignity" is the key word that separates these two stories. Common infidelity and promiscuity are not issues in Hemingway's world, and whenever it is present (*The Sun Also Rises, The Garden of Love*) it is handled indirectly, unlike Carver, who deals with these undignified issues head on. The heroic acceptance in Marjorie that this is the end is quite a contrast to the drunken, suicidal response of Holly, who also knows (like Marjorie) what her life lacks: that dignity—she does, after all, tell Duane, "I used to be a proud woman," while Marjorie lets Nick know she does not need his help to push the boat onto the water, she is just fine without him. Hemingway's characters never lose their self-respect, a trait that has no relevance in Carver's world, where characters are compulsive, self-indulgent, and have little backbone or self-control. Moreover, they're no indication that they're even "expected" to have these virtues, to live up to any social code and script that Hemingway's characters have been brought up to believe. This is the difference of times: Hemingway's pre-WW I and II America and Carver's post-Vietnam, post-sexual revolution America. The way the characters act towards each other can certainly raise the issue of social and economic milieu, even ethics, of a two different Americas— the values, upbringing, mores, and social decorum of both are many worlds apart, the definitions of pride and dignity possesses two different meanings. Nick and Marjorie can still, post-break-up, cross paths in social settings and hold their chins high and interact without anger or pain; for Duane and Holly, the end of something seems to be the end of everything.

NOTES ON A FEW MORE SENTENCES

The following further sentences I will comment on have hit my heart and my memory—but mostly my heart, for it is the heart that matters most in fiction.[21]

> "My heart is broken," she goes. "It's turned to a piece of stone. I'm no good. That's what's as bad as anything, that I'm not good anymore" (105).

Holly is serious, this is what brings her to a suicidal realization, that she to move to Nevada "or kill myself" (106). He tries to make her believe otherwise, telling her she is still "a proud woman" (105) which only annoys her, insisting it is true and telling him, "Just don't argue with me" (106).

This passage reminds me of Liv; when we started our relationship, she forewarned me that she would break my heart, that she was not, deep down, a good person.

I asked, "Do you like breaking hearts?"

She replied, "No, but I always seem to."

I said, "Then stop."

She said, "I don't know how."

Sure enough, she broke my heart, many times. And I kept going back; I kept going back until I finally told her, "Look, my heart has been broken by you so many times that it can't be fixed, it's broken for good, all you can do now is toss it out in the trash and kill me." She didn't listen, she continued to hurt me; moreover, I did not listen, I

---

[21] Or, to quote Gordon Lish from his private fiction workshops: "With your words, you are looking for a new heart."

did not heed her warning, she told me this would happen and there was no stopping it but love made me—what—deaf, blind, stupid. It happens to all of us. It happened to Duane and Holly, certainly. Like me, Duane is not listening to his wife. It is not until the end that he realizes what she says is true, she is broken to the point that she cannot be fixed. The last sentence claims: "In this too, she was right." She has told him the story about how she envisioned the two of them as an elderly couple, being nice to lost strangers who come by asking for directions, as they were in Yakima. Now that will never be. That future will never be, and she is broken and unfixable, Duane knows this now and there is nothing he can do. He has not looked at their future, and now he knows there isn't one—at least not the one Holly had hoped for.[22] During the process of his revelation, he does know he is going to lose her. "I get down on my knees and start to beg" (106). She seems to find this insincere, but it makes her cry and want to drink more. Carver has a narrator get on his knees, in repentance, in a later story, "Intimacy," about a man who visits his ex-wife. In is obviously an autobiographical piece about Carver and his first wife, but the characters do not have names, they could be Duane and Holly fifteen-to-twenty years later.

This post-*Cathedral* text, the last of a handful that Carver wrote before his death in 1988, is included in *Where I'm Calling from*; it reads more like a monologue

---

[22] I am reminded of a moment when I lived with Tara, whom I lived with for almost three years. A couple in their late 50s moved into the apartment next door to us. They were gray, quirky, and not that bright in my asinine opinion. "That's us in the future," Tara said; "that's exactly what we'll be like." Six months later, she moved out.

than a short story. It starts by saying he "has some business out west anyway, so I stop off in this little town where my former wife lives" (331). He is trying to deflect his visitation with the word "anyway." As the story, or monologue, progresses, it becomes clear he has wanted to see his ex-wife for some time; he *needs* to, and the "business" is simply an excuse to do what he's been thinking of doing for a while. As I stated, there is every indication that "Intimacy" is autobiographical—the unnamed narrator is a writer, he sends his ex-wife published stories, book reviews, and interviews. Carver's ex-wife, Maryann Burke Carver, has stated that although all the depictions of her has caused her to "lose my identity" her reaction to "Intimacy" was to say "god bless him" because he showed the weaknesses and flaws of his male characters (himself) as much as the women (her).[23] "She says I've caused her anguish…made her feel exposed and humiliated" (331). This is what Maryann Burke Carver means by losing her identity—being "exposed" to the world in published writing means the fronts, the masks, and public faces people create are washed away, and possibly embarrassing human frailties she would prefer to keep secret are now municipal.

Former spouses, when getting together after a period of time, tend to fall back into the people they used to be. She, this nameless ex-wife, is trying to move on from that trap.

> She says she wishes I'd forget about the hard times, the bad times, when I talk about back then. Spend some time on the good times, she says. Weren't there some good times? She wishes I'd get off that other

---

[23] From Sam Halpert's interview in *…When We Talk About Raymond Carver.*

subject. She's bored with it. Sick of hearing about it. Your private hobby horse, she says. What's done is done and water under the bridge, she says. A tragedy, yes. God knows it was a tragedy and then some. But why keep it going? Don't you ever get tired of dredging up that old business?

She says, Let go of the past, for Christ's sake. Those old hurts. You must have other arrows in your quiver.... (331-332).

Despite her admonishment, it is she who starts bringing up the "old hurts." The narrative starts to become hers, as she flings accusations and shameful events, one after the other, talking so fast he cannot get a word in. She says, "We were so intimate I could puke. I can't imagine ever being that intimate with somebody else" (333). She then indicts him of being on a "fishing expedition" and "hunting for *material*"24 for his writing (333). He does not deny it.

It was like I *stopped living*. My life had been going along, going along, and then it just stopped. It didn't just come to a stop, it screeched to a stop. I thought if I'm not with anything to him, well, I'm not worth anything to myself or anybody else either. That was the worst thing I felt. I thought my heart would break (334).

We see how she sounds just like Holly, recounting the despair of her past. In her monologue within his monologue, she is self-actualizing, using him as a springboard for her own self-psychoanalysis. She wants him to think she is stronger for it, she is better off; but she actually regrets be-

---

24 Carver's emphasis.

ing vulnerable; this angers and disgraces her. She tells him "you held me up for display and ridicule in your so-called work […] for any Tom or Harry to pity or pass judgment on" (335).[25] After all this yelling and recollection of pain and betrayal, she tells him to go but what he does is fall to his knees and grab at the hem of her dress. He is on his knees and cannot move; this surprises both him and her. She realizes he wants forgiveness. Her tone changes, referring to him as "honey" and "stupid" in the same sentence (336). She contends that she forgives him, although it is obvious she does not…she cannot.

She wants him to go, she is nervous, not only by what he is doing but her new husband will be home soon and she does not want to try to explain what he might see—this ex-husband on his knees, clinging to her, on the verge of a breakdown. To get him to leave, she grants him license to continue on, to write about their lives, to "tell it like you have to […] and forget the rest" (337). She says he is "free" (337). Is this what he came here for? Clemency and autonomy to carve out the intimacies of their failed marriage in the name of American fiction? Walking away from the scene, he treads through "piles of leaves" (337). There are leaves everywhere, falling, so many that he thinks "somebody ought to get a rake and take care of this" (337).

The leaves are all his issues of the past; the little things that have fallen, out of his reach and control; matters he cannot let go of. His desire to "get a rake" represents his

---

[25] Mary Anne Burke tells Halpert that after the success of *Will You Please Be Quiet, Please?* and the National Book Award nomination, she was uncomfortable with having her life scrutinized and criticized. "It felt as if I were in a fishbowl and yet not really seen" (101).

wish to gather up all his issues and remove them with one swoop. The problem here, of course, is that he says "somebody" should do it, rather than himself. He knows his ex-wife will eventually have to come out and do the job, but he will not be there, so what good will this be for him? He will always have piles of leaves until he gets his own rake. Then again, they are not his leaves, they are hers.

PLACE IN CARVER'S CANON

The final sentence I would like to comment on is: "There was this funny thing of anything could happen now that we realized everything had" (108). What more *can* happen? They are at the breaking point, Hemingway's "moment of truth," and the true, the anything that can happen, is that neither of them knows what will happen. The script of their lives has come to an end, it has been taken over by a different writer. It is both frightening and exciting for Duane and Holly, because maybe this had to happen, maybe this drama was the metaphorical two-by-four across the head they both needed, to wake up from the daze that was their lives, lives going nowhere. "We knew our days were numbered" (108).

"Anything can happen" also refers to Carver's life and career. When "Gazebo" was first published in a small literary magazine, his career was still uncertain, his first book was out and he was still teaching, struggling with income. He was at a point where anything could happen—he could go big, become a master of American fiction, or he could sink into obscurity, a mere footnote in twentieth-century literature. In Carver's canon, "Gazebo," is not his best known work, or taught in high schools and colleges the way "Popular Mechanics," "So Much Water So Close to Home," "A Small, Good Thing," "Fat" and "Cathedral" are. It is one of his finest works not only as an example of twentieth-century minimalism, but as a work that contains every theme, or "obsessions"[26] as Carver preferred to call them: issues of drinking, infidelity, poverty, marriage, memory, and an uncomfortable feeling of being lost in the American landscape of the time, "homeless, jobless," as the flap copy of *What We Talk About When We Talk About Love* states, "bewildered Americans in hysterical motion from one spoiled place to another. There are people who are rooted in dislocation,"[27] bewildered, baffled and gone

---

[26] Halpert, in his interview with Jay McInerney, comments on how Carver "regarded his success as an unexpected gift" (46); McInerney replies: "That was an endearing trait of Ray's. Right up to the very end, he was flabbergasted by each new honor" (46).

[27] As written by Gordon Lish. No editor has written dusk jacket copy like Lish. "In Raymond Carver's fiction," he contends, "the door is always open because someone is always leaving — and the TV is always going because it is safer to look at television than at people." The copy also comments on "the stunned custodians in 'Gazebo,' whose names alone are far more burden than they can manage." I have tried to figure out what Lish means by this, and have not come up with an answer, which is why I place this in note rather than in the body of the essay. It is a matter for another critical work, perhaps by a different Carver scholar. Webster's definition of "holly" is "any of a genus of trees and shrubs; *especially* [...] with spiny-margined evergreen leaves and usually red berries often used for Christmas decorations." Females born near Christmas are often named Holly, in Old English tradition, and literature's best-known Holy is Holly ("Holiday") Golightly in Truman Capote's *Breakfast at Tiffany's*. Carver's Holly is not like Capote's, other than Capote's ran away from her simple life on a farm to reinvent herself in New York. Carver's Holly does want to run away to Nevada and start her life over. "Duane" is of Irish and Gaelic origin, its meaning "dark" or "swarthy." A search for "Duane and Holly" on

astray by life and love, these are the elements in "Gazebo" that speak to my own experiences, the components of my memory, and so is at the top of the list of Carver's most important work.

Google.com does not brig up any interesting allusions, but does hit a short paper by Karen Bernardo about "Gazebo." Bernardo notes that Holly, like the tree she is named after, "wants roots, and instead has been granted the job of managing the affairs of transients in a home that isn't a home and doesn't even belong to her."

12.

"I'VE SEEN SOME THINGS": PARENTAL GROTESQUE AND THE SEX LIVES OF MOM AND DAD

Two stories from *What We Talk About When We Talk About Love* are about a first-person narrator coming to terms with a parent's sexuality: "Mr. Coffee and Mr. Fixit"[28] and "Sacks." In "Mr. Coffee and Mr. Fixit," the narrator's mother is a widow. "My dad died in his sleep, drunk, eight years ago" (20). The first sentence is classic Carver: "I've seen some things" (17). He explains that he

> was going over to my mother's to stay a few nights.
> But just as I got to the top of the stairs, I looked and
> se was on the sofa kissing a man [...] That's one of
> the things I've seen [...] My mother is sixty-five. She
> belongs to a singles club. Even so, it was hard. I

---

[28] A longer version of the story titled "Where is Everyone?" was published in the Spring 1980 issue of *Triquarterly* and Carver's collection, *Fires: Essays, Stories, Poems*. I am quoting from this version because *What We Talk About When We Talk About Love* is the standard volume used when studying Carver.

stood with my hands on the railing and watched as
the man kissed her. She was kissing him back (17).

Knowing that his mother is sleeping with this man who is
not his father troubles him. It's in the past, he says, "but
back in those days, when my mother was putting out, I
was out of work. My kids were crazy, and my wife was
crazy. She was putting out too (17).[29] He is a man facing a
life is coming apart—unemployed, with a widowed mother
and a cheating wife, the reader almost expects that—
despite the calm, understated tone of the sentences—this
man is going to snap and do something violent. Seeing his
mother kiss this man might send him over the edge as he
thinks abut his wife with other men. He remembers one of
the men his wife was cheating with, and how he had another lover, "a twenty-two year old named Beverly" (19)
which left his wife rejected and hurt. "I used to make fun
of him when I had the chance" (19) he concludes.

In "Sacks," the narrator is a traveling regional book
sales rep, estranged from his father. On a business trip, he
learns a disturbing truth about why his parents divorced. "I
want to pass along to you a story my father told me when I
stopped over in Sacramento last year" (37) be begins. He
meets his father for a drink; his father feels the need to
confess something he's never told anyone. At the age of

---

[29] For the sake of curiosity and how different versions differ, the same
passage from "Where is Everyone?" in *Fires* reads: "...during those
days, when my mother was putting out to men she'd just met, I was
out of work, drinking, and crazy. My kids were crazy, and my wife
was crazy and having a 'thing' with an unemployed aerospace engineer she'd met at AA" (173).

fifty-five, he had an affair with a thirty-year-old "Stanley Products woman [...] your mother was always buying from her, a broom, a mop, some kind of pie filling" (39). The woman comes by one day when the narrator's mother is not there, and his father answers the door. The father explains:

> One thing's leading to another [...] Well, I kissed her then. I put her head back on the sofa and I kissed her, and I can feel her tongue out there rushing to get into my mouth. You se what I'm saying? A man can go along obeying all the rules and then it don't matter a damn anymore" (42-43).

The father is still just as surprised by the memory of what he'd done as when he was doing it—and the narrator, well, his comment is, "I didn't say anything at all" (43). The father goes on about how affairs always mess things up—eventually the other woman's husband walks in on them, and instead of becoming violent "he got down on the floor and cried" (45). The narrator's mother finds out and leaves his father, the dirty secret of their family's past.
  Like the narrator in "Mr. Coffee and Mr. Fixit," the revelation of the infidelity is flabbergasting, leaving both narrators numb; the past they knew is no longer true. After the father confesses, he leaves and "that was the last I've seen of him" (45). The narrator is indifferent; he never knew who his father really was, just as the other narrator does not know who is sexually active sixty-five-year-old mother is. Parents, it is revealed, no matter what their age,

are just as flawed and in need of sexual connection as the confused offspring are.

13.

RE: "A SERIOUS TALK"

" A Serious Talk," from *What We Talk About When We Talk About Love,* sums up the Carver's entire career. It is a grim, sad story and contains every theme and motif found in Carver's collected fiction—the failed marriage, the drunken exploits, the other lover waiting in the wings, the children having to deal with a broken family, smoking and drinking, doing regrettable things, and not saying the words that are inside the heart, but do not seem to be able to come out of the mouth.

In "A Serious Talk," Burt is a man estranged from his wife and family; it is the day after Christmas and the night before he got drunk and botched things up (again). He returns seeking forgiveness from his wife but she will not give it to him. She is seeing another man, which he reacts to in quiet anger and jealousy, and a bit of alcoholic sadness. He wants to have a "serious talk" with her, he believes this penultimate talk will fix everything that is wrong, but he cannot come up with the proper words.

> He was not certain, but he thought he had proved something. He had hoped he had made something clear. The thing was, they had to have a serious talk soon. There were things that needed talking about, important things had to be discussed (113).

Many critics have contended that the real power of Carver's short fiction lies in what is *not* said rather than what *is*. The reader, going along with the narrative, knows what the characters *need* to say to each other to smooth out the misunderstandings and the rough spots of their lives; the reader becomes frustrated, identifies with what is happening, hopes the characters will do the "right" thing.

"A Serious Talk" exhibits this quandary of what is not, and should be, spoken. All Burt does is muse about this *talk* they must have; he tells her this, he thinks on it, but it never happens. Instead, he pours another drink and smokes another cigarette, motifs in many Carver's stories, where the characters are too preoccupied with the physical objects that give them a buzz to deflect from what is really going on in their lives. He hopes "he had made something clear," but nothing is clear because nothing has been uttered—or, often, the *wrong* things have been said, accompanied by unfortunate acts (such as Burt leaving the pie he dropped out in the driveway, discarded and invisible as far as he cares). He is not sincere when he apologizes to his wife. "Sorry isn't good enough," she tells him (108). She seems to be waiting for him to do, say, "the right thing," yet knows he will not, cannot. Perhaps she wants him to fall to his knees and beg clemency, in Yeats, the way the narrator does in a later Carver story, "Intimacy." For all his drunken antics, he should, and maybe she would react the way he wants her to, maybe she will believe he truly is sorry. Why else would she allow him back into the house, back into the family's life, when she vowed to not let him hurt her and the kids again?

> "Do you remember Thanksgiving?" she said. "I said then that was the last holiday you were going to wreck for us. Eating bacon and eggs instead of turkey at ten o'clock at night" (108).

Yet, here he is again, she has allowed him back, perhaps hoping things will change.

This is endemic of most, if not all, Carver characters— if only they would show sincerity, speak up, things might change. Pride or indifference becomes the obstacle. With Burt, he is too preoccupied with getting in the way of his wife's boyfriend rather than making amends. This is typical in stories like "Gazebo," from the same collection, where the husband and wife are too busy drinking and re-hashing the past rather than discussing the present problem that is ruining their marriage. In "Are You A Doctor?" and "Are These Actual Miles?" from *Will You Please Be Quiet, Please?,* both the male protagonists never tell their wives what it is that is truly troubling them—ether perceived infidelity, shame of poverty, or loss of human connection, they *seem* on the verge of telling their wives what is going on inside their hearts, but they never do, and so nothing changes, and misunderstandings happen. Story after story, we find that this is the core issue of Carver's fiction; and so "A Serious Talk" is the best flagship text that can be pointed to and said: "Here is the overall problem with Carver's men and women...."

"There were things that needed talking about, important things had to be discussed." This sentence not only sums up Carver's oeuvre, but possibly many people's lives. I know it does mine. This is why many readers identify with Carver's stories quite easily.

14.

RE: "WHAT WE TALK ABOUT WHEN WE TALK ABOUT LOVE" A.K.A "BEGINNERS"

When *The New Yorker* published Raymond Carver's unedited version of "What We Talk About When We Talk About Love" under its original manuscript title, "Beginners," a great deal of debate and chatter was epidemic in the literary community, in print, online, and in many blogs: was the original better than the edited version, the version Carver fans and critics know so well? Was Lish the perspective villain, forcing his brand of literary style on Carver's true intentions, or did he improve Carver's work by cutting it down to "what matters"?[30] Two months prior to *The New Yorker* edition, Carver's widow, Tess Gallagher, went public with her desire to republish all of her late husband's stories, from his second collection, in their unedited, original manuscript form. Publisher Knopf, holder of the copy-

---

[30] In a letter dated January 17, 1971, Carver writes to Lish about his editing: "Listen, something you said a long time ago, the thing itself is what matters. Is true, in the end."

right to *What We Talk About When We Talk About Love*, did not want to pursue this.[31] *The New Yorker* published, on-line only, a version of the story showing what lines were deleted and what Lish added, borderlining the deft editor's hand and the clever collaborator's contribution.

In this explication I present the first three paragraphs of "What We Talk About When We Talk About Love" that comprise the first paragraph of "Beginners" and defend Gordon Lish's editorial choices. The first excerpt is from the 1981 collection; the second is from *The New Yorker*.

> My friend Mel McGinnis was talking. Mel McGinnis is a cardiologist, and sometimes that gives him the right.
>
> The four of us were sitting around his kitchen table drinking gin. Sunlight filled the kitchen from the big window behind the sink. There were Mel and me and his second wife, Teresa—Terri, we called her— and my wife, Laura. We lived in Albuquerque then. But we were all from somewhere else.
>
> There was an ice bucket on the table. The gin and the tonic water kept going around, and we somehow got on the subject of love. Mel thought real love was nothing less than spiritual love. He said he'd spent five years in a seminary before quitting to go to medical school. He said he still looked back on those years in the seminary as the most important in his life (137).

---

[31] In the *New York Times* article, "The Real Raymond Carver: Expansive or Minimal?", Knopf editor Gary Fitsketjon questions why she wants to "rewrite history").

My friend Herb McGinnis, a cardiologist, was talking. The four of us were sitting around his kitchen table drinking gin. It was Saturday afternoon. Sunlight filled the kitchen from the big window behind the sink. There were Herb and I and his second wife, Teresa—Terri, we called her—and my wife, Laura. We lived in Albuquerque, but we were all from somewhere else. There was an ice bucket on the table. The gin and the tonic water kept going around, and we somehow got on the subject of love. Herb thought real love was nothing less than spiritual love. When he was young he'd spent five years in a seminary before quitting to go to medical school. He'd left the Church at the same time, but he said he still looked back to those years in the seminary as the most important in his life.

Why was "Herb" changed to "Mel"? Aside from legal reasons, best left to a publisher's house consul, does it matter what a character is named in the overall meaning of a story? I will argue that Mel sounds more pleasing with its alliterative value to "McGuinnis." Say both names out loud several times—*Mel* is more friendly, more relaxed (apologies to all Herbs who may read this), considering the setting: friends sitting around drinking and talking. This is subjective but the mind of an editor always is, and I will say Lish was thinking what the reader would find more pleasant-sounding for a name. Some may say this is proof that Lish's editing was too aggressive; I contend that Lish's motive was to make the text more "friendly" to the reader.

Next, Lish breaks the opening paragraph into three, which loosens the text up, rather than the block of words

Carver initially chose as introduction. It fits better with the amount of dialogue and action that is in the story. Each paragraph does start a new idea—the introduction of Mel, the introduction of the rest of them, and the introduction of alcohol and what these people are doing together.

Changing "there was Herb and I" to "Mel and me" is more colloquial, and as we read the story, it is apparent that the proper "and I" does not fit with the narrator's personality and syntax. "And I" would make the narrative feel forced and self-conscious ("Herb and me" does not have a pleasing alliterative ring to it either). In the next sentence, "then" is added after Albuquerque, ending the sentence. "Then" establishes that the story, being told as a memory, was a while ago, and the narrator is recounting it in another city and setting. "Then" also suggests that things, presently, are different between these people, as one might say, "We were good friends *back then*." The next sentence "but we were all from somewhere else" is more to the point as its own sentence, not with the comma in transition. There is a quiet half-beat difference between a comma and a period. This is a sentence that, when read out loud, has a better textual flow.

Lish deletes "when he was young" and "he'd left the Church" because it is obvious that, in the past, he was younger, and quitting the Church is discussed later in the story. To say "when he was young" is redundant—everyone is younger than they were when it comes to the past. Does it "matter" here? No. Since this is all established later, the revelations of love and youth and what people when they are younger would have less effect if revealed in the opening.

The same criteria for the deletions and additions by Lish hold true throughout the entire story. The two versions are not widely different overall, it is the simple and small details of sentence structure and what information is important, or not, that "matters." While Carver's original is useful as a study in the evolution of a text and the relationship of writer and editor, it is neither "improved" nor "better"—it shows where Carver once *was*, and how he arrived to what he now *is*. Lish, it is apparent, helped Carver find his correct path and the publication of the original merely serves as the blueprint—Carver was the architect with the designs, Lish was the construction foreman with the tools and means to build.

15.

WHY DO YOU ASK?
THE INTERROGATORY STORIES
OF RAYMOND CARVER

Raymond Carver published eight stories with titles that ask a question, what Arthur M. Saltzman, in *Understanding Raymond Carver*, contends to be "urgent demands for justification" (47) by the characters. While it has come to light that a few of these stories had their titles changed by Gordon Lish, not all of them were[32], especially "Will You Please Be Quiet, Please?"[33] William L. Stull deems *Will You Please Be Quiet, Please?* "obsessively interrogative" in the *Diction-*

---

[32] A 1970 story, "Cartwheels," was later re-titled "How About This?" Perhaps this early success of "Will You Please" influenced him to use question marks in other titles, which has now become a Carver trademark—so much that writers who title their short fiction with question marks are often mindful that they may appear to be imitating the late, great Raymond Carver, icon and institution of twentieth-century American letters.

[33] The story had the same title when first published in the small press journal, *December*, in 1967 and in the 1976 McGraw-Hill book.

ary of Literary Biography. Seven of the eight inquiry stories are found in that book; in *What We Talk About When We Talk About Love*, there is just one: the lead story, "Why Don't You Dance?" There are none in *Cathedral*.

The story title is often uttered by one of the characters, usually a query posed to the protagonist/narrator. I will explicate each question in chronological order, as appearing in print in the collections. In "Are you a Doctor?" a woman calls the wrong number but engages in a conversation with the protagonist Arnold.[34] She finds Arnold interesting to talk to and wants him to come to her apartment and visit. Arnold is married but is curious who this woman is, and he seems to need something to happen in his dull life, with a lackluster marriage. The woman has a child who is sick and she asks Arnold if he is a doctor and can he help. Carl and Mary are a married couple in "What's in Alaska?"[35] She has a job interview that will require her to move to Fairbanks, Alaska, to which Carl replies, "I always wanted to go to Alaska" (78). Their friends think such a move is crazy, but for Carl and Mary, they have no roots or prospects where they are, and a move is welcome; they are not stuck in one place like those around them. In "What Do You Do in San Francisco?" a postal carrier becomes mildly obsessed about where a young couple has

---

[34] Carver revisits the idea of the misdialed phone call having an effect on the life of the person being called in "Whoever Was Using This Bed," one of the handful of stories he write before his death.

[35] In "Gazebo," when the wife, Holly, is ready to leave her husband, Duane, for his infidelity, she says she is going to Nevada and he asks, "What's in Nevada?" The story could have easily been titled that and would have worked just as well as "Gazebo."

come from, what their lives were like before moving into a house on his route. He muses,

> You hear rumors. At different times I heard he was an ex-con on parole who come [sic] to Arcata to get out of an unhealthy San Francisco environment [...] Another story was that he committed a crime and was hiding out here (116).

"Why, Honey?" takes the epistle form: a woman writes to a man who knew her son, now dead, and offers her tender memories of a child with hard luck. "How About This?" is about a relationship that appears to be on the verge of falling apart until the woman tells the man, "we have to love each other [...] We'll just have to love each other" (194) as if they have no choice, this is their fate and there is no way out. In "What Is It?" (re-titled "Are These Actual Miles?" in *Where I'm Calling from*) a couple have filed for bankruptcy and "the car needs to be sold in a hurry, and Leo sends Toni out to do it" (208). Toni knows that if she goes alone, dressed nicely, she will attract the attention of the men at the used car lots and get a better deal. She tells him, "I'll have to have to have dinner or something [...] that's the way they work, I know them. But don't worry, I'll get out of it" (209). She doesn't, and he suspects she had sex with the used car salesman who asks him, "Are these actual miles?" about the car.

"Will You Please Be Quiet, Please?" is centered on a past indiscretion of Marian, who is married to Ralph. At a party a few years back, Marian left the gathering with a friend, Mitchell Anderson, to buy more alcohol before the store closed. Ralph has suspected all along that more than harmless kissing went on that night; he has bottled it up and now he wants answers and verification of his worst fears: that his loving wife may have cheated on him. So she tells him that when she drove the store with Mitchell, they parked, he kissed her breasts: "He said shall we have a go at it?" (237)

In the last of these interrogatory tales, "Why Don't You Dance?" is about a man selling off his possessions from a former life, when he was happily married. He sells his stuff to a young couple; he gets them drinks, plays records, and watches the two dance, remembering his better years when he once knew love.

Why do some authors choose to use questions in their titles? Some find it confronting, a method of not being coy or employing elusive literary tricks. In Carver's work, they are question that require answers, the demand for justification that Saltzman contends is urgent; even if the answers prove to be futile and uncomfortable, the characters (and the reader) cannot evade the interrogation and have to respond, or in some cases, comply, such as when Ralph asks Marian if she "will please be quiet, please?" when she tries to defend her act of infidelity and save her marriage. As for why the older man does not dance, he cannot go back to what he once was, and Carl and Mary cannot provide a satisfying answer about what is in Alaska because their friends refuse to understand.

16.

DECIDING ISSUES: RAYMOND CARVER ON THE BODY OF THE INFANT AND THE ENTRAPMENT OF FATHERHOOD

NOTE: This chapter and the next are variations on the same study of "Popular Mechanics." In this one, my method is standard comparative criticism with another Carver story, "The Father," relating it to issues of fear and fatherhood, popular themes in emerging Men's Studies. In the next chapter, I examine "Popular Mechanics" from several critical perspectives, and mostly relate the story to events I my own life as well as my own philosophies of life. There is some overlap of sentences.

"The Father" and "Popular Mechanics" are Raymond Carver's shortest works of prose and, at heart, concern men who feel oppressed, trapped in their domestic situation and role as father. Both stories also focus on the body, and body parts, of an infant. In "Popular Mechanics," the man is in the process of escape; in "The Father," he is faced with the epiphany that he "doesn't look like anybody" (42) and has no true identity. A mere two pages each, less than 500 words, "The Father" is included in Carver's collection, *Will You Please Be Quiet, Please?* and "Popular Mechanics" in his second, *What We Talk About When We Talk About Love*.[36]

"The Father" finds a man surrounded by women: his wife, their three daughters, and the grandmother; they are all doting over the new baby boy. He never speaks, does not utter a single word; merely listens to them all from the kitchen, "sitting at the table with his back to them" (42). The females comment on the baby's body parts: eyes, lips, nose, arguing about whom the child looks like and which

---

[36] An early version, with slight differences in sentence structure at the beginning and the end, is called "Mine" in *Furious Seasons*. In *Where I'm Calling from* it is re-titled "Little Things" without any changes in the text. Later in his career, Carver revised a number of stories, or returned them to their previously edited form along with their original titles. There is significant documentation and debate as to the extent that Gordon Lish, Carver's friend and editor at *Esquire* and Knopf, edited and re-titled Carver's work, and if the editorial hand was reaching into the gray zone of actual co-authorship. In D.T. Max's article, "The Carver Chronicles," he notes that Lish had been publicly confessing to what in essence may have been ghostwriting, but he was not being taken seriously and: "Seven years ago, Lish arranged for the sale of his papers to the Lilly Library at Indiana University. Since then, only a few Carver scholars have examined the Lish manuscripts thoroughly. When one [Brian Evenson] tried to publish his conclusions, Carver's widow and literary executor, the poet Tess Gallagher, effectively blocked him with copyright cautions and pressure." Max examined the archive papers himself and found evidence, on edited Carver manuscripts, that this assertion looked to be true. Max interviewed Lish in New York: "We sat across from each other at his kitchen table and I asked him what had happened. 'I don't like talking about the Carver period,' he said, 'because of my sustained sense of his betrayal and because it seems bad form to discuss this [...] [and] puts me in an absolutely impossible light [...] I can only be despised for my participation.'"

one of them he loves the most. A daughter, Phyllis, claims "he really loves Daddy because Daddy's a boy too!" (41). There is another man in the house now, among these five women; there is no indication whether the father is happy about this or not, and what he appears to be brooding about, sitting there at the table. Most likely, he is pondering on the economics of having another life to look after, another mouth to feed; burdened with this responsibility, he will probably have to work more hours or get a second job. William L. Stull claims this story is Kafkaesque and "charts the collapse of a young husband's identity" ("Raymond Carver Remembered" 466). It is "a textbook piece on existential fear and trembling" ("Beyond Hopelessville" 3). The father's epiphany of "not looking like anybody" other than the *pater familias* the girls know is a harsh slap in the face; he realizes that the world sees him as nothing more than a provider, a man who takes care and feeds, not a man with any hopes or dreams, or even a past; hence, he is "nobody" which leaves him "white and without expression" (42).

"Popular Mechanics" is an ugly piece and difficult to digest. A couple's relationship is in the final moments of deterioration; they argue, continue to hurt each other with words, attempt to possess the last thing linking them together—the baby—and apparently injure the infant in the process. Carver never describes the assumed violence; he infers it, and that is exactly what makes it a *horror* story: he leaves it to the reader's imagination what, in the end, happens, or how "the issue was decided" (125). One assumption, in Norman German and Jack Bedell's "Physical and Social Laws in Raymond Carver's 'Popular Mechanics'", is that "the grim conclusion, the breaking or dislocating of the baby's arm, occurs in the reader's mind, after some thought" (258). What does or does not transpire after the last sentence depends on the reader's personal experience, background, and philosophy to conjure up. In Stuart Karatany's review of the Turkish translation of *What We Talk About When We Talk About Love*, he writes, "'Popular Mechanics' is a horrendous piece about a man deserting a woman—he wants to take their baby with him and in the scuffle that ensues each pulls the baby very hard by one arm" (131). Karatany, from his cultural viewpoint, assumes that the man is "deserting" her when Carver neither states nor implies such. She could be kicking him out of the home for all we know, just as we do not know whether these two people are married or not. He refers to the infant as "the baby" and she tells him: "You're not touching this baby" (124). She doesn't say "our" or "my"—"this" and "the" baby is simply an object between them, like an ex-couple fighting over who gets the TV or radio. We have absolutely no clue who these two people are, what their relationship status is, and what kind of past they have shared. We do not know what has happened that has him packing suitcases. He *could* be reacting to her having an affair or he could be leaving her for someone else.[37] Such is the case with minimalist fiction: without biographical information or explication of characters' feelings and

---

[37] Maryann Burk Carver, in her memoir *What It Used to Be Like*, writes of an incident very similar to this scene when Carver was ready to leave and take their daughter with him after he believed she was having an affair. He says she can keep their son, as if this is an equitable split of communal property. "Over my dead body will you take my little girl," she tells him (122).

thoughts, the reader is left with the task of filling in the blanks.

German and Bedell's take on the story is that "the baby's welfare is not the 'issue'" and "Carver seems to be retelling and altering the story of Soloman and the two mothers" (259).[38] The couple is engaged at one-upping the other, who will walk away the victorious. In *The Carver Chronotope*, G.P. Lainsbury writes: "Both father and mother are determined to take something away from the ruins of their marriage, and the baby is the thing which will prove to the world that he or she is the better, more caring parent"(132-33). The final sentence is a "gruesome pun" (133) in that the infant and the argument are both at "issue." An infant is not going to remember what happened—it is harrowing, however, to consider what the baby will have to go through when older, discovering the truth about the sustained injury from the past. What if the incident leaves residual physical discomfort throughout this child's life? One could rightly assume that this baby will grow up to be a bitter, angry, and confused adult, who may have a subconscious embedded memory of the distress and agony when "the issue was decided."

The infant's gender is never identified. If it were either a boy or girl, it would become subject. The boy in "The Father" is also objectified: he is almost like a new toy for the three sisters to play with as they touch his chin and other body parts; the grandmother is preoccupied with the child's "little arm! So fat. And those little fingers!" (41).

---

[38] Arthur M. Saltzman agrees with this in *Understanding Raymond Carver*: "[He] provides no Solomon to arbitrate between his two battling, embattled parents" (95).

She also thinks "he has his grandfather's lips" (42) while the mother views him as perfect and healthy, with no concerns that there is now a fourth child to take care of. She seems happy with her life and marriage, unlike the woman in "Popular Mechanics" who says she is glad her partner is leaving—this is probably something she has been thinking about for a while (perhaps leaving herself). She accuses: "You can't even look me in the face, can you?"(124) This likely is not the first time she has said that, and could be a quality of his personality that bothers her: when they talk, when things get serious, he can never look at her, either out of embarrassment or apathy. The opening paragraph describes the weather outside; the sun is setting and it is getting dark. "But it was getting dark on the inside, too" (124). Whatever the collected elements of unhappiness and anger are, they have culminated into a darkness that is about to explode into domestic violence and child abuse.

Both fathers are weary of the pressure that comes with having children to support; although in "Popular Mechanics" he intends to take the child and burden himself with the prospect of becoming a single father. Another economic issue is at hand: if he does leave with the baby, how is he going to take care of it alone? He will need someone to watch over the child when he goes to work, when he spends time with friends. Obviously, he is not taking this matter into consideration, all he seems concerned with is the moment; and in that moment, he wants to deny his spouse/partner of her identity of motherhood. He knows that taking the baby would only serve to hurt her. As Lainsbury contends, each wants to prove they are the better parent, that one is the victim and one is the oppressor; despite whatever happened to cause the couple to fight, no matter who is at fault, the man is determined to look like the victim, the single father who had to rescue his child from a bad mother.. If he succeeds in getting out of this perceived ensnarement, he may be jumping into a bigger trap; he finds himself in a Catch-22 situation unless he is willing to make a clean break (although he would probably have to pay child, and maybe spousal, support down the line). In "The Father," when he turns around to look at the five females and his new son, his "existential fear and trembling" is that he has no way out, he is facing his jailers and his prison cell. Both men, then, are prisoners of the economic realities of being family men.

The economic factors of Carver's short fiction have labeled him a blue-collar, working class writer. In an interview with John Alton, he says that "most of the people I've written about in the early books are the working poor, and I know that life very well indeed [...] It's been said that I portray people struggling in a society that is oppressing them" (11). It is this very oppression that has caused one father to flee, committing an act of violence, and brings about the other father's collapsed identity. The result is that the oppression escalates, and both men find themselves in a new prison. One father has to deal with the social, psychological, and legal stigma of injuring his infant, the other has to live with the knowledge of his nobody-ness: he has no way to change that, it all looks hopeless to him. Each man has to face a new horror: one from action, the other from non-action; they have stepped into the excruciating, painful traps of contemporary domestic life.

17.
DOMESTIC VIOLENCE AND CHILD ABUSE IN AMERICAN SHORT FICTION:

or:

WHAT WE FIGHT ABOUT WHEN WE FIGHT ABOUT THINGS

> That's part of what I was talking about when I was talking about things "too tedious to talk about."
> ---Carver[39]

"**P**opular Mechanics" is Carver's shortest, most violent and disturbing work of prose.[40] A mere two pages, it is found in *What We Talk About When We Talk About Love* and re-titled "Little Things"[41] in *Where I'm Calling from*. It is an ugly piece

---

[39] See Simpson, Mona.

[40] The story also seems to be quite popular when assigned in college literature courses. Running a Google search, more than a dozen pre-written essays on either "Popular Mechanics" or "Little Things" pop up for sale from various term paper services.

[41] A version called "Mine" is included in *Furious Seasons and Other Stories*.

and difficult to digest, a "slice of life" about a couple's relationship in the final moments of deterioration. They argue, continue to hurt each other with words, attempt to possess the last thing linking them together—the baby—apparently injuring the infant in the process. Carver never depicts the assumed violence; it is between the lines; he infers it, and that is exactly what makes this story a *horror* story: he leaves it to our imagination what, in the end, happens, or how "the issue was decided" (125).

One assumption is that "the grim conclusion, the breaking or dislocating of the baby's arm, occurs in the reader's mind, after some thought" (German and Bedell 258). What does or does not transpire after the last sentence depends on the reader's personal experience, background, and philosophy to conjure up. In Stuart Karatany's review of the Turkish translation of *What We Talk About When We Talk About Love*, he writes, "'Popular Mechanics' is a horrendous piece about a man deserting a woman—he wants to take their baby with him and in the scuffle that ensues each pulls the baby very hard by one arm" (131). Karatany, from his cultural viewpoint, assumes that the man is "deserting" her when Carver neither states nor implies such. She could be kicking him out of the home for all we know, just as we do not know whether these two people are married or not—there is a child, but is he the father? Is she the mother? She could have had the child with another man, and vice versa. He refers to the infant as "the baby" and she tells him: "You're not touching this baby" (124). She doesn't say "our" or "my"—"this" and "the" baby is simply an object between them, like an ex-couple fighting over who gets the TV or radio. The point is, we have absolutely no clue as to who the hell these two people are, what their relationship status is, and what kind of past they have shared. We do not know what has happened that has him packing the suitcases. He *could* be reacting to her having an affair;[42] they *could* be watching a friend's or family member's child. They could be brother and sister. Anything is possible.

There are numerous categories of critical criteria when approaching these few words about human relations—a scholar could examine the text utilizing social, anthropological, economic, feminist, political, and psychoanalytical theories. In this essay, I will consider them all, and take into account the personal: what does a story like this mean to me, in context with my experiences, memories, feelings, and philosophy?

Norman German and Jack Bedell co-authored the four page "Physical and Social Laws in Raymond Carver's 'Popular Mechanics'" in 1978. Their take on the story is that "the baby's welfare is not the 'issue'" and "Carver seems to be retelling and altering the story of Soloman and the two mothers" (259). Arthur M. Saltzman agrees with this in *Understanding Raymond Carver*: "[He] provides no Solomon to arbitrate between his two battling, embattled parents" (95). When spouses and couples dissolve their relationships, matters are always complicated when there is a child or children involved. While "spouses divorce each other, but they do not divorce their children" (Blaisure and

---

[42] In fact, Maryann Burk Carver, in her memoir *What It Used to Be Like*, writes of an incident very similar to this scene when Carver was ready to leave and take their daughter with him after he believed she was having an affair. He says she can keep their son, as if this is an equitable split of communal property. "Over my dead body will you take my little girl," she tells him (122).

Gleasler) and all too often, in today's landscape of failed unions, "children can become pawns...and are often used as objects through which one parent can get back at the other" (Thayer and Zimmerman). Books, studies, seminars, brochures, and specialized areas of psychology and counseling have been devoted to this topic. Various academic studies and the news on television claim the percentage rate of divorce in the United States increases each year; children caught in the middle create a new set of complications. Two acrimonious people tend to abide colossal umbrage, fury, and disappointment toward each other when challenged with collaborating on one of the most complicated tasks in the world: child-rearing in a co-parent agreement.[43] To say that the social situation can be

---

[43] A former friend of mine left her husband a year after marriage, taking their infant with her. Her husband came home after work—on April Fools Day, no less—and found that the apartment empty, his wife and child gone, a note was waiting for him. Needless to say, he was not happy about being abandoned; his revenge, upon agreeing to give her sole custody, was to forbid her from leaving the city with the child. If she wanted to move away, he would take custody. This was arranged and settled in the divorce proceedings in court. She was not willing to give her baby to him; however, she was an actress and had dreams of making a career in Hollywood. She was twenty-three and knew she had to move to Los Angeles soon, before she became too old to chase the film acting career she'd dreamt of since she was a teenager. She was never able to do this, however. She worked as a cocktail waitress and nine-to-five in offices, acting in the occasional small theater production and never getting the attention, the recognition, she craved and desired—the sort of ego-boosting only being in a Hollywood or independent film would provide. Time went by fast and the next thing she knew she was in her thirties and it was too late to start from square one in the movie business—that was for women ten years younger than her, and 99% of those would never get anywhere in one of the most competitive professions in the world. To "cope," she started to

"painful" for all parties concerned would be an ironic understatement for "Popular Mechanics." In the dissertation, *The Carver Chronotope*, G.P. Lainsbury writes: "Both father and mother are determined to take something away from the ruins of their marriage, and the baby is the thing which will prove to the world that he or she is the better, more caring parent"(132-33). (Lainsbury automatically assumes they are married.) The final sentence is a "gruesome pun" (133) in that the infant and the argument are both at "issue." Older children who find themselves in the middle of divorced and vindictive parents are deeply affected by what they witness and hear; there is damage to their

---

drink a lot and swallow pharmaceuticals; she would get too drunk and sleep with married men or men she worked with, regretting it in the morning with a pounding hangover. She constantly thought of suicide and had to take various dosages of anti-depressants. The choices she made, when young, haunted her every hour of the day. One time, she said to me, "I always wonder what my life would be like had I not screwed the wrong guy, got knocked up and married; I wonder what my life would be like if I had gone to L.A. when I was nineteen and really went for it. Maybe I would have failed, I don't know. Maybe I would've been a big famous movie star by now; I'll never know." For her, the issue will never be decided. This is a perfect example of how one single life choice can set an entire future down a path one never thought was in the fixed stars of their fantasies. Many men and women are doing time in jail and prison for making rash, unwise choices in a single unfortunate moment. We can say this is the case with the man and woman in "Popular Mechanics"—their heated argument, and the end result, will follow them for the rest of their lives (to say nothing of the child); after all, if the baby is indeed severely injured as implied, they will both most likely be charged with child abuse and be sent to jail, their baby left in the care of either a family member or a foster home. Fiction has the convenience of ending on the last page, that world comes to a close and the repercussions never have to be dealt with. In actual life, decades of pages are left to be written after "the end." There is no escape from bad deeds done. It is a prison.

growth into adulthood—this is contemporary psychother-apy's allowance of blame for an adult's shortcomings, and neuroses, to the parents and any inflicted childhood trau-mas. An infant is not going to remember what happened and what was said—it is harrowing, however, to consider what the baby in this story will have to go through when discovering the truth about the sustained injury during in-fancy. And what if the incident leaves residual physical discomfort throughout this child's life? Taking a psycho-analytic approach, one could rightly assume that this baby will grow up to be a bitter, angry, and confused adult, who, during hypnotherapy, will remember the distress and agony when "the issue was decided."

When couples argue and fight, the core problematic is-sue is that one, or both, is not getting what is needed or wanted in life; they are dissatisfied and probably heartbro-ken that their dreams are slipping away from them. For young parents, goals and ambition tend to be set aside or abandoned when the majority of free time is occupied with the care and feeding of another; otherwise, the parents are out working jobs to make money so that they *can* care and feed. Again, with Carver offering no background informa-tion about the man and woman, there is no data to deter-mine why they are both unhappy. She says she is glad that he is leaving—this is probably something she has been thinking about for a while (perhaps leaving herself). She accuses: "You can't even look me in the face, can you?"(124) This likely isn't the first time she's said that, and could be a quality of his personality that bothers her: when they talk, when things get serious, he can never look at her, either out of embarrassment or apathy. The opening paragraph describes the weather outside, with "snow…melting into dirty water" (124). The sun is setting and it is getting dark. "But it was getting dark on the inside, too" (124). Carver is not referring to the couple's home but the couple's hearts, souls. Whatever the collected elements of unhappiness and anger are, they have culminated into a darkness that is about to explode into domestic violence.

Another common element for the dismay in marriages and relationships is money. Couples fight over finances, it seems to be a fact of life. "When a couple has any problem, it's because of a power imbalance," says Donna Laikind, a marriage and family therapist, quoted in an article, "The Top Five Things Couples Fight About", adding: "Money is not seen as the commodity that it should be. It's fraught with layers and layers of meaning." The lack of money can cause people to become scared, insecure, confused, transforming into anger. A person may see their partner as the nexus of the economic woes; perhaps they are unemployed or do not want to work, or spend too much money, or cannot get a better job to bring in more money. Looming bills, hunger, and insomnia are good enough reasons for a person to pack up their clothes and leave, as the man in this story is doing. He could be weary of the pressure that having a partner and child to support brings upon him, although he intends to take the child and burden himself with the prospect of becoming a single father. Another economic issue is at hand: if he does leave with the baby, how is he going to take care of the baby alone? He will need someone to watch over the child when he goes to work, when he spends time with friends. Obviously, he is not taking this matter into consideration—all he seems concerned with is the moment; and in that moment, he wants to deny his spouse/partner of her identity of motherhood.

The economic factors of Carver's short fiction have labeled him a working class writer. The blue-collar existence and literature converge in the Carver universe, not unlike Steinbeck and Bukowski. His characters are often poor, unemployed, worried about money or arguing about money.[44] In an interview with John Alton, Carver comments:

> Most of the people I've written about in the early books are the working poor, and I know that life very well indeed [...]I've been accused — and praised — for taking, or not taking, a social stand in my work. It's been said that I portray people struggling in a society that is oppressing them, and so this society — the society we're living in — is corrupt, it's bad, the system has failed us, and so on. And on the other hand, I have been accused of making "political" statements that are harming the republic in some way by not putting a happy face on things... (11-12).

Lainsbury's responds to the Alton interview by stating "Carver's writing is based upon onto-theological concepts such as authenticity, honesty and integrity of purpose, and

---

[44] Sometimes the first sentence explains the economic situation. From "They're Not Your Husband": "Earl Ober was between jobs as a salesman." From "Collectors": "I was out of work." From "Vitamins": "I had a job and Patti didn't." In "Are These Actual Miles?" a car needs to be sold fast to get money; in "Elephants," the narrator is going broke because numerous members of his family keep asking for money.

the communication it attempts concerns the emotional life of its characters rather than an effort on the part of its creator to make sense of the world they inhabit" (14). In Megan D. Snyder's unpublished dissertation, "Author as Ethnographer: The Merging of Genres in Raymond Carver's and Thomas Pynchon's Texts," Carver is seen as an anthropologist, and his fiction "function[ing] as ethnography" or qualitative field notes that reveal the working class in the 1960s and 1970s, examining "the dominant and dominated codes of American culture" (152). Indeed, Carver's work can be construed as commentary of lower and middle class American life, habit, and mores in the later half of the 1900s, just as Bret Easton Ellis is the spokesperson for pop culture America in the '80s and David Foster Wallace for the '90s. The fiction writer as cultural anthropologist, it seems, is a new field of study waiting to bloom on the outer fringes of the academy.[45]

---

[45] To expand on this theory, it is my contention that William T. Vollmann and Dave Eggers—both luminaries of contemporary American literature—are practitioners of ethnography. Vollmann's work is quite autobiographical and Eggers is best described as memoir and biography. From an ethnographic approach, Vollmann's *Butterfly Stories* works as field notes for socio-economics in Thailand, and what citizens there must do to survive, and how that survival is culturally acceptable or unacceptable (prostitution, for this book). In *The Atlas, Rising Up and Rising Down*, and *Poor People*, Vollmann reports on his travels around the world and, using a participant-observer methodology, writes about other cultures, attempts to understand the complexities of these other cultures, and asks a multitude of questions, the answers serving as data. For instances, he asks numerous interview subjects when do they believe violence is justified and why do they believe they are poor. Further, Vollmann's *Seven Dream* series works ethnographically on the present cultural and social conditions of Native American Indians, tracing historical events, in quasi-fictional form, that lead to how Native Americans live today. As for Eggers, his memoir *A Heartbreaking*

Both camps in feminist and men's studies could raise various social and behavioral, and perhaps gender, issues about "Popular Mechanics." Why is the sex of the child never identified, and is only "the baby"? If the baby were either a boy or girl, that would humanize the child, when, in the context of this story, it is mere object. From a feminist theoretical approach, this story serves as criticism on the male desire to dominate women: he demands that he takes custody of the baby, without consideration to her mental health, need, and well-being. He knows that taking the baby would only serve to hurt her. As Lainsbury contends, each wants to prove they are the better parent, that one is the victim and one is the oppressor; despite whatever happened to cause the couple to fight, no matter who is at fault, the man is determined to look like the victim, the single father who had to rescue his child from a bad mother, a courtroom tactic common in custody hearings when parents fight over the children and seek to make the other "look bad" in public record. Within the discipline of men's studies, this could be a good case for men's rights issues: why *shouldn't* he have the baby? This is his child, after all. Why, within the practices of contemporary society, is it always expected that the woman will be left with the child, and should *have* the child? It is common that the

---

Work of Staggering Genius, works on various levels of ethnography: a contemporary family without traditional parental figures (Eggers is left to raise his younger brother when their parents die), San Francisco culture, and the booming magazine publishing scene of the 1990s when anyone could create a publication on their desktop computers. Computer and desktop publishing culture is a valid subject of study for any anthropologist; likewise, Eggers' *What is What* is a biography of a Sudanese refugee trying to fit into American society, dealing with the clashing of cultures and social mores.

courts often award custody to the mother over the father—but does that necessarily mean a child is better off with one parent over the other, notwithstanding the gender?

This little story has had, as mentioned before, three different titles. Why is it called "Popular Mechanics," the title of a slick science magazine? Carver scholar Steven J. McDermott, at his blog *Storyglossia*, suggests the title

> emphasized science, as well as technology-based home improvement projects, many of which were do-it-yourself.
>
> Several interpretations are suggested: The couple treat the dissolution of their marriage as a do-it-yourself home improvement project, and that such dissolutions are "popular"; in the sense that they are common, the norm; and the baby is treated as a toy/mechanical device rather than as a living breathing child. The title also gets the imagination working on the physics—the *mechanics*—of two adults pulling with all their might on the baby's arms.

There are minor revisions from the version "Mine" in *Furious Seasons* when it became "Popular Mechanics" (as "Little Things" it remains the same) that are worth noting. The last sentence of the first paragraph was originally: "It was getting dark, outside and inside" (92) and became the more menacing: "But it was getting dark on the inside, too" (124). There are subtle changes in the final sentences between the two versions; in a story like this, a single word, an altered punctuation, makes a world of difference.

> She felt her fingers being forced open and the baby going from her. No, she said, just as her hands came loose. She would have it, this baby whose

chubby face gazed up at them from the picture on the table. She grabbed for the baby's other arm. She caught the baby around the wrist and leaned back. He would not give. He felt the baby going out of his hands and he pulled back hard.

He pulled back very hard. In this manner they decided the issue. (*Furious Seasons* 93)

She felt her fingers being forced open. She felt the baby going from her.

No! she screamed just as her hands came loose. She would have it, this baby. She grabbed for the baby's other arm. She caught the baby around the wrist and leaned back.

But he would not let go. He felt the baby slipping out of his hands and pulled back very hard.

In this manner, the issue was decided. (*Where I'm Calling from* 154)

McDermott believes that the rewrite of the last sentence "reinforces the lack of control the parents have because in fact they aren't deciding anything," although the "issue" has now been decided for them, via their animosity towards each other. "Neither of them," McDermott concludes, "give in and the *mechanics* of the baby's bones relative to the strength of the adults pulling is presumably what decides" where their relationship is going to take the next step.

If Carver is the father of twentieth-century minimalist fiction, as some maintain, "Popular Mechanics" is his calling card. In *Minimalism and the Short Story: Raymond Carver, Amy Hempel, and Mary Robinson*,[46] Cynthia J.

---

[46] Carver, Hempel and Robison were all edited and published by Gordon Lish at Knopf, which brings up a valid question: is Gordon Lish the se-

Whitney Hallet argues: "Minimalist short fiction is part of that design of the short story as defined by Poe, characterized by Chekhov, and refined by Hemingway which eventually emerged fully formed in the fiction of Carver" (15). For some critics, minimalism is a four letter word, and for some writers, a scarlet letter. Carver did not care being pigeon-holed as such. Michael Trussler, in "The Narrowed Voice: Raymond Carver and Minimalism," attests that critics are "so captivated…with the term's (supposed) ability to provide precise and final demarcation, that it seems paradoxical to discover the myriad of widely diverse cultural activities jointly labeled by the 'minimalist' aesthetic….the term is used pejoratively, a rapid dismissal of an artwork, often made more on moral than stylistic grounds" (23). "A critical appreciation of the term," counters Hallet, "minimalism is not a negative literary evaluation…[but] an elaborate arrangement of vernacular and trope that appears as concrete details which reflect complex states of being and which correlate with elements of the universal human condition" (47). Steven J. McDermott disputes: "'Popular Mechanics' is a metafictional rejoinder to the critics who've labeled him a minimalist, which reflects a major concern of Carver's when he published *Where I'm Calling from*: He wanted to present his work in a broader perspective, illustrate that the *minimalism*—a label which he rejected—was just a technique used

---

cret father of minimalism? The obvious similarities in the style of other writers edited by Lish are hard to ignore. For example, Barry Hannah's *Ray* and *Captain Maximus*—acquired and edited by Lish for Knopf—resemble Carver's sentence structure and style. Hannah's style, prior to having Lish as an editor, is quite different. Or is this actually Lish's style when we talk about style?

in some stories, not the defining characteristic of his work." Needless to say, at less than 500 words, "Popular Mechanics" has inspired thousands of words of discourse and colloquia (this essay adding to that body of work).

I previously stated that "Popular Mechanics" is ugly and difficult to read—it is similar to watching two people having a heated argument in a restaurant or a park; you want to turn away and ignore them, pretend they aren't here and not be a witness to the terrible ways people treat each other when there is no more love and only fear. Perhaps we are reminded of our worst moments, when we have acted the same way; perhaps we witnessed our parents or grandparents interact in the same manner, so seeing others engaged in this behavior brings back painful childhood memories. For me, all of the above apply, and this is what makes "Popular Mechanics" difficult on a personal level. It is exactly that discomfort which has motivated me to write this essay. I have seen friends treat each other the way the man and woman in this story treat each other. I must be honest and admit I have acted this way, fought this way, with women I have been in relationships with, when things went sour and south. My parents, who were teenagers when I was born, fought a great deal when I was a child. There was physical violence. When I was six or seven, I woke up and heard my parents arguing. I was thirsty and wanted some milk. I got out of bed and saw my mother standing at the end of the hallway. I went to tap her on the leg and ask for milk. She quickly stepped out of the way and I felt a thud hit me on the chin. My mother and father went silent, staring at me with abject dreadfulness. "Oh my God," my mother said, grabbing me. I saw a beer can on the floor. My mother touched my face and there was blood on her hands. My father had thrown the beer can at my mother; she moved away so she wouldn't get hit and I was hit in the chin instead. The opened edge of the can cut my flesh open. I didn't feel anything because I had no idea what happened. When I saw the blood, and felt the open wound on my chin, my mind and body flooded with enormous pain and I screamed, I cried—my parents rushed me to the emergency room and the doctors stitched up my chin. They had to sedate my father because he was acting like a madman, hitting the walls with his fists, screaming, "What if I had hit him in the eye? What if I had taken his eye out? Why did I do that? What is wrong with me?!"

I still have that scar on my chin today, thirty-four years later. People always ask, "How did you get that scar?" I never tell the truth. I don't want people to think my father was a child abuser. I still remember the anguish, though, and that night—the moment of impact, beer can to chin, has followed me everywhere I go, a mark on my body, and every time I see a beer can, I am reminded of what my father did, and how the issue was decided.

18.

FINAL QUOTES

unaccountably we are alone
forever alone
  ---Bukowski

There was a time
I would've died for love.
  ---Carver

BIBLIOGRAPHY

Alton, John. "What We Talk About When We Talk About Literature: An Interview with Raymond Carver." *Chicago Review* 36 (Fall 1988):4-21.

Anon. "The Top Five Things Couple Argue About." Sixwise.com.

Anon. "Interview with Dan Fante." *Lummox Journal.* http://www.lummoxpress.com/lummoxpress/id10.hml

Ask the Dust. Robert Towne, dir. Paramount Classics, 2006.

Barfly. Barbet Schroeder, dir. Cannon Film Distributors, 1987.

Bernardo, Karen. "Raymond Carver's 'Gazebo.'" Storbites.com.

Bethea, Arthur M. "Raymond Carver's Inheritance from Ernest Hemingway's Literary Technique." *The Hemingway Review* 26.2 (Spring 2007): 89-104

Blaisure, Karen R. and Margie J. Geasler. "Children and Divorce." URL: http://www.aamft.org/families/Consumer_Updates/Children andDivorce.asp

Bukowski, Charles. *Crucifix in a Deathhand.* New Orleans: Loujon Press, 1965.

-----.*Cold Dogs in the Courtyard.* New Orleans: Loujon Press, 1965.

-----. *Love Is a Dog from Hell.* Santa Rosa, CA: Back Sparrow Press, 1977. Santa Rosa, CA: Back Sparrow Press, 1977.

-----. *Betting on the Muse.* Santa Rosa, CA: Back Sparrow Press, 1996.

-----. *Post Office.* Santa Barbara: Black Sparrow Press, 1971.

-----. *Factotum*. Santa Barbara: Black Sparrow Press, 1975.

-----. *Love Is a Dog from Hell: Poems 1974-1977*. Santa Barbara: Black Sparrow, Press, 1977.

-----. *Women*. Santa Barbara: Black Sparrow Press, 1978.

-----. *Ham on Rye*. Santa Barbara: Black Sparrow Press, 1982.

-----. *The Movie: "Barfly."* Santa Rosa: Black Sparrow Press, 1987.

-----. *Hollywood*. Santa Rosa: Black Sparrow Press, 1989.

-----. *The Captain is Out to Lunch and the Sailors Have Taken Over the Ship*. Santa Rosa: Black Sparrow Press, 1998.

Buford, Bill. "Editorial." *Granta* #8.

Capote, Truman. *Breakfast at Tiffany's*. NY: Random House, 1958.

Carver, Maryann Burk. *What it Used to Be Like*. NY: St. Martin's Press, 2006.

Carver, Raymond. Carver, Raymond. *Will You Please Be Quiet, Please?* New York: McGraw-Hill, 1976.

-----. *Furious Seasons and Other Stories*. San Barbara: Capra Press, 1977.

-----. *Fires: Essays, Poems, Stories*. Santa Barbara: Capra Press, 1983.

-----. *What We Talk About When We Talk About Love*. NY: Knopf, 1981.

-----. *Cathedral*. NY: Knopf, 1984.

-----. *Where I'm Calling from*. NY: Atlantic Monthly Press, 1988.

Cooper, Stephen. *Full of Life: A Biography of John Fante*. NY: North Point Press, 2000.

-----, ed. *The John Fante Reader*. NY: Ecco, 2002.

Delany, Samuel R. *The American Shore*. Elizabethtown, NY: Dragon Press, 1978.

DeLillo, Don. *Falling Man*. NY: Scribner's, 2007.

Disch, Thomas M. *334*. London: MacGibbon & Kee, 1972.

Eggers, Dave. *A Heartbreaking Work of Staggering Genius*. NY: Simon and Schuster, 2000.

-----. *What is What*. San Francisco: McSweeney's Books, 2007.

Factotum. Brent Hamer, dir. IFC Films, 2006.

Fante, Dan. *Chump Change*. Northville, MI: Sun Dog Press, 1998.

-----. *Mooch*. Edinburgh, Scotland: Canongate Books, 2000.

-----. *Corksucker.* East Yorkshire, England: Wrecking Ball Press, 2004.

-----. *Short Dog.* Northville, MI: Sun Dog Press, 2006.

Fante, John. *Wait Until Spring, Bandini.* Boston: Houghton Miflin, 1977.

-----. *The Road to Los Angeles.* Santa Barbara: Black Sparrow Press, 1985.

-----. *Ask the Dust.* NY: Stackpole Sons, 1937. Bantam, 1954.

-----. *Dreams from Bunker Hill.* Santa Barbara: Black Sparrow Press, 1982.

Federman, Raymond. *Critifictions: Postmodern Essays.* Albany: SUNY Press, 1991.

Gentry, Marshall Bruce and William L. Stull. *Conversations with Raymond Carver.* Jackson: University Press of Mississippi, 1990.

German, Norman and Jack Bedell. "Physical and Social Laws in Raymond Carver's 'Popular Mechanics.'" *Critique* 29.4 (Summer 1978): 257-60.

Giles, Marta. "Teacher: A Memoir of Raymond Carver." URL: http://www.nd.edu/~ndr/issues/ndr7/gies/gies.html

Hallett, Cynthia J. Whitney. *Minimalism and the Short Story: Raymond Carver, Amy Hempel, and Mary Robinson.* Lewiston, NY: Edwin Mellen Press, 1999.

Halpert, Sam, ed. *...When We Talk About Raymond Carver.* Layton, UT: Gibbs Smith, 1991.

Hannah, Barry. *Ray.* NY: Knopf, 1980.

-----. *Captain Maximus.* NY: Knopf, 1985.

Harrison, Russell. *Against the American Dream: Essays on Charles Bukowski.* Santa Rosa, CA: Black Sparrow Press, 1994.

Hemingway, Ernest. "The End of Something." *In Our Time.* NY: Charles Scribner's Sons, 1925.

-----. *The Sun Also Rises.* NY: Charles Scribner's Sons, 1927.

-----. *The Garden of Eden.* NY: Scribner's, 1983.

Hemmingson, Michael. Rev. of *Critifictions: Postmodern Essays* by Raymond Federman. *Critique: Studies in Contemporary Fiction* 36.4 (Summer 1995): 281-82.

-----. *Drama.* NY: Blue Moon Books, 2002.

-----. *Gordon Lish and His Influence on 20th Century American Literature.* NY: Routledge, 2009.

-----. *Carver's Women: Role, Place, and Identity of the Feminine in Raymond Carver's Short Stories.* Jackson, NC: McFarland & Co., 2009.

Holmes, John Clellon. *Go.* NY: Thunder's Mouth Press, 2002.

Jewel. *A Night Without Armour.* NY: HarperCollins, 1998.

Kaiser, Hellmuth. "Kafka's Fantasy of Punishment." In Kafka, Franz. *The Metamorphosis.* NY: Bantam Classics, 1986.

Karatany, Stuart. Rev. of *What We Talk About When We Talk About Love. Journal of American Studies of Turkey* 3 (1996): 131-32.

Lainsbury, G.P. *The Carver Chronotope: Inside the Life-World of Raymond Carver's Fiction.* NY: Routledge, 2004.

Lentricchia, Frank. *After the New Criticism.* Chicago: University of Chicago Press, 1980.

-----. *Lucchesi and the Whale.* Durham, NC: Duke University Press, 2001.

Lish, Gordon. *Dear Mr. Capote.* NY: A William Abrams Book/ Holt , Rinehart and Winston, 1983.

Lynn, Kenneth. *Hemingway.* NY: Simon and Schuster, 1987.

Leypoldt, Gunter. "Raymond Carver's 'Epiphanic' Moments." *Style.* Vol. 35, No. 3, Fall 2001: 531-49.

McCaffery, Larry and Sinda Gregory. *Alive and Writing: Interviews with American Authors of the 1980s.* Urbana: University of Illinois Press, 1987.

----- and Michael Hemmingson. *Expelled from Eden: A William T. Vollmann Reader.* NY: Thunder's Mouth Press, 2004.

McDermott, Steven J. "Title Your Way To Meaning." *Storyglossia* 8 February 2004. URL: http://www.storyglossia.com/blog/archives/2004_02_08_archive. html.

-----. "The Art of Revision." *Storyglossia.* 13 February 2004. http://www.storyglossia.com/blog/archives/2004_02_08_archive. hml

Madsen, Michael. *Burning in Paradise.* San Diego, CA: Incommunicado Press, 1998.

Max, D. T. "The Carver Chronicles." *New York Times Magazine* 9 August 1998.

Mullen, Bill. "A Subtle Spectacle: Televisual Culture in the Short Stories of Raymond Carver." *Critique: Studies in Contemporary Fiction.* Vol. 39, Winter, 1998.

Nabokov, Vladimir. *Pale Fire.* NY: G.P. Putnam's Sons.

Ronell, Avital. *Crack Wars.* Lincoln, NE: University of Nebraska Press, 1991.

Saltzman, Arthur. *Understanding Raymond Carver.* Columbia: U. of South Carolina Press, 1988.

Simpson, Mona. "The Art of Fiction LXXVI." *The Paris Review* 88 (Summer 1983):192-221.

Snyder, Megan D. "Author as Ethnographer: The Merging of Genres in Raymond Carver's and Thomas Pynchon's Texts." Dissertation. U. of Alaska, Fairbanks, 1999.

Stull, William L. "Beyond Hopelesville: Another Side of Raymond Carver. *Philological Quarterly* 64.1 (winter 1985): 1-15.

-----. "Raymond Carver Remembered: Three Early Stories." *Studies in Short Fiction* 25.4 (fall 1988): 461-69.

-----."Raymond Carver." *Dictionary of Literary Biography Yearbook 1988.* Ed. J. M. Brook. Detroit: Gale, 1988: 199–213.

Thayer, Elizabeth and Jeffrey Zimmerman. *The Co-Parenting Survival Guide.* Oakland: New Harbinger, 2001.

Tompkins, Jane. "Me and My Shadow." *The Intimate Critique: Autobiographical Literary Criticism.* Ed. Diane P. Freeman *et al.* Durham, NC: Duke University Press, 1993: 23-40.

Trussler, Michael. "The Narrowed Voice: Raymond Carver and Minimalism." *Studies in Short Fiction* 31 (Winter 1994): 23-37.

Vollmann, William T. *Butterfly Stories.* NY: Grove Press, 1993.

-----. *The Atlas.* NY: Viking, 1996.

-----. *Rising Up and Rising Down.* San Francisco: McSweeney's Books, 2003.

-----. *Poor People.* NY: Ecco, 2007.

-----. *Riding Towards Everywhere.* NY: Ecco, 2008.

Woodward, Ron. "Behind the Mask? Don Fante Interview." http://www.burningshorepress.com/interviews/behind_the_mask.php

ABOUT THE AUTHOR

MICHAEL HEMMINGSON writes books in every possible
genre he can: literary, western, SF, horror, noir, autobiography, erotica, narrative journalism, gonzo journalism, cultural anthropology, critical theory, critifiction, ethnography, sociology, and many other modes of academia including post-postmodern and post-colonial treatises. And private eye yarns. And film and TV studies. And smut. He
also writes plays and screenplays. He has two independent
feature films out: *The Watermelon* (LightSong Films) and
Stations (Hemlene Entertainment). He has produced, di-
rected, and written plays in San Diego and Los Angeles
for the Fritz Theater and The Alien Stage Project. He lives
in Southern California, going back and forth from Hollywood to San Diego.

CPSIA information can be obtained
at www.ICGtesting.com
Printed in the USA
FSOW02n0725071016
25855FS